FABULOUS HARBOURS

a sequel to

BLOOD

Michael Moorcock

FABULOUS HARBOURS

a sequel to

BLOOD

MILLENNIUM
An Orion Book
LONDON

The right of Michael Moorcock to be identified as the author of
this work has been asserted by him in accordance with the
Copyright, Designs and Patents Act 1988.

This edition first published in 1995 by
Millennium
An imprint of Orion Books Ltd
Orion House, 5 Upper St Martin's Lane
London WC2H 9EA

A CIP catalogue record for this book is available
from the British Library

ISBN: (Csd) 1 85798 408 0
(Ppr) 1 85798 409 9

Printed and bound in Great Britain by
Clays Ltd, St Ives plc

For
Ackroyd & Sinclair,
Master Brewers

So, come, Rose, I shall lead thee
  To the flaming fields of May,
When scarlet kisses silver
  As the sunset flows away.
And then Rose I shall fly thee
  Through the gorgeous jade-blue day,
Where, moored in fabulous harbours,
  Hide the dreams of yesterday.

Ernest Wheldrake,
'*Soli Cantare in Periti Arcades*'
1874

Acknowledgements

The White Pirate first appeared in *BLUE MOTEL*,
   edited by Peter Crowther, 1994.
The Black Blade's Summoning first appeared as
   The White Wolf's Song in *TALES OF THE
   WHITE WOLF*,
   edited by Edward E. Kramer, 1994.
Lunching With the Antichrist first appeared in
   SMOKE SIGNALS,
   edited by the London Arts Board, 1993.
The Affair of the Seven Virgins first appeared in
   THE TIME CENTRE TIMES,
   edited by John & Maureen Davey, D. J. Rowe and
   Ian Covell, 1994.
The Girl Who Killed Sylvia Blade first appeared in
   GOLDEN NUGGET,
   edited by M. Moorcock, 1966.
Crimson Eyes first appeared in
   NEW STATESMAN & SOCIETY,
   edited by Steve Platt, 1994.
No Ordinary Christian first appeared in *TOMBS*,
   edited by Kramer & Crowther, 1995.
The Enigma Windows first appeared in
   NEW STATESMAN & SOCIETY,
   edited by Steve Platt, 1995.
The Birds of the Moon first appeared in
   NEW STATESMAN & SOCIETY,
   edited by Steve Platt, 1995.

All other material is original to this book, copyright
   Michael and Linda Moorcock, 1995.

Contents

Introduction

I take little credit for what is good or interesting about these stories. They were told to me, mostly at second hand, by Edwin Begg, who was present when they were told to him. He described the pleasant anticipation he felt when hearing that Jack Karaquazian and Mrs Colinda Dovero were coming to visit. That, he said, was when the best stories were aired. Nobody felt they would be disbelieved.

This book is, the reader will see immediately, no direct sequel to the events in Blood, though it refers to the same characters and concerns. Neither can I promise a return to the conventions in the final novel of the sequence The War Amongst The Angels. The stories are familiar enough, in their essentials, but they tell of a slightly better world, I suspect, than ours, unlike that which Jack Karaquazian and Mrs Colinda Dovero left behind to go there.

Many of the indigenous inhabitants of this world would argue for its imperfections, but newcomers see it as a form of Paradise where society has proceeded at a somewhat slower and more dignified pace towards justice and equity. It is a world where the further you travel from London, the more exotic it becomes. Whereas Edwin Begg's world is pretty familiar to the average Londoner, the world of Ulrich von Bek is I would guess familiar only in fiction. These are the romantic places and events produced in the twentieth century imagination and they reflect, I suppose, our yearnings as well as the disappointed hopes of the post-war years which created so many social reforms, but failed to achieve what almost all reform movements promise to do and that is restore a perfect past to a perfect present.

I believe our visions reveal our motives and identities. I also believe that one day our visions of a perfect society will be subtle enough to work. Here, for the time being, is a vision of some imperfect world that is somewhat better than our own, perhaps the most we can hope for if we survive the next couple of centuries.

Michael Moorcock,
Lost Pines,
Texas
March 1995

1. *the retirement of jack karaquazian*

Home from his travels in Chaos Space and reunited in the First Ether with the love of his life, Colinda Dovero, Mr Jack Karaquazian determined that he would no longer live the uncertain life of a professional gambler and chose instead, with Colinda's enthusiastic agreement, to open a small casino on Las Cascadas, that island principality where more than one British sailor had retired and which remained a popular resort for the English-speaking tourists who admired the island's population, living with several religions, cultures and political doctrines, in cheerful harmony.

Al Vaquero Enmascarado, their establishment, was named in honour of a famous old resident of the island, Ferdinand Faust. Under his mother's surname, as Warwick Begg, Faust wrote the famous 'Masked Buckaroo' series, so popular with readers between the two world wars. Thanks to many B-Westerns made from his stories in Hollywood and France, Faust was a wealthy man. He had moved to Las Cascadas from Italy at the time of the Lombardian War of Secession and had become a respected member of the island community. Many Masked Buckaroo fans came to his villa, now a museum, every year. Living in a studio at the back of the main house, he was known to enjoy an occasional bottle of the Oban and had a singular taste for Ackroyd's Vortex Water, which had to be imported from Sinclair's Whitechapel Distilleries in special containers. Any fan who brought a bottle of Ackroyd's was welcome for the several hours it would take Faust to consume it. He was flattered by the couple's choice of his title and received a small percentage of the profits for its use. The place became very popular with tourists and Mr Karaquazian and Mrs Dovero were able to retire from active involvement in their enterprise, spending much of their time travelling to the more exotic regions of Europe and Africa, occasionally taking the long Zeppelin journey to India or China and becoming enthusiasts for Japan and her culture.

[3]

Several times a year Jack and Colinda would visit the small apartment they kept just behind Peter Jones's – an area of astonishing tranquillity in the heart of Chelsea known as Peabody Gardens, untouched by developers and the home of working families who had been there since the time of Blake. Sir Sexton Begg, a friend made in Las Cascadas, sometimes offered them his flat in Sporting Club Square if their own place was not available. But even if they did not stay in Sporting Club Square they always made it their business to visit, for they were great friends with several other Beggs, including the patriarch himself, Squire Begg. At ninety-four years old and not a bit frail, Squire Begg was always glad of news from his beloved Las Cascadas. He had owned a villa there but had been forced to sell it when his nephew Barbican engineered the famous crash of BBIC and ruined almost everyone he knew.

Jack and Colinda especially enjoyed their visits when Rose von Bek, their oldest friend, was also able to be there. The family possessed a vast treasury of experience, equal to the couple's own, and so it was a pleasure to exchange tales with people who were not a bit discomforted by the unusual, the bizarre and the fantastic aspects of the modern world. They shared an interest also in quirks of human character and the peculiar stories which resulted from them.

After so many wild adventures in the multiverse, which left him with unique psychic scars, Jack Karaquazian was content to sit of a warm autumn evening near the central tennis courts of Sporting Club Square, listening to the sound of ball on racket and smelling the late roses, swapping stories with his friends the Beggs, whose ancestor had built this square in all its fantastic, fin-de-siècle elegance.

On one particular such evening, with the red sun slowly flooding the sky and the branches of the great Duke's Elm spread as if in triumph against it, Jack Karaquazian, Colinda Dovero, Countess von Bek, Commander Albert Begg, Sir Sexton Begg, Aunt Poppy Begg and her companion, Miss Sipp, recollected the story of the White Pirate with such enthusiasm that even their various children came to listen, which meant a certain stylistic reticence on the part of Albert Begg, the chief teller, and a few minor evasions in the version recorded here . . .

2. *the white pirate*

Introductory

We visit Las Cascadas again, learning a little more of Begg Mansions and Sporting Club Square. Our main tale concerns Captain Horace Quelch, the infamous White Pirate and self-advertised 'Last Christian Corsair on the Barbary Shore', and his oddly suited paramour, the Rose, a famous adventuress – how they first met, serving by some fluke an identical cause, while running guns into Africa. Yet this is not our central theme, which addresses the mystery of Quelch's unadvertised cargo, known from Port o' Spain to Ghana's Corsair Coast as 'The Dead Man's Chest', and carrying with it an enormous weight of legend and myth . . .

CHAPTER ONE

The Rover's Return

One night a trim schooner came into Las Cascadas Bay, dropping her anchor and her bilges to the vociferous disgust of the port's residents crowding their buff-coloured terraces and lush balconies to peer down on dark emerald-blue waters at that pale gold ship drifting in moonlight as if she had just sailed in from fairyland.

The schooner was, the rumour ran, crewed entirely by beautiful women. Don Harold Palimpest had seen them through his glass – and he could read a book on the moon with that powerful tool.

An official visitor to the island republic, Captain Albert Begg, RN, was paying a courtesy call to the British Honorary Consul, Don Victor Dust, whom he had discovered to be a man of enormous literary education and enthusiasm, with a tolerant knowledge of life to match Begg's own, making Don Victor the best company Begg had experienced in his years of seven oceans, five continents and a hundred secret missions. They sat smoking on Dust's balcony, facing directly across the bay which was warmed, even at midnight, by light from the bars and restaurants along the harbour, and the almost-full moon shining directly overhead. From here they could watch the newcomer and speculate about her in the luxury of their reclining chairs.

Captain Begg opined that the schooner was too clean for a trader and her canvas too tidy for a private yacht. He thought she could be a youth-training vessel out of Gibraltar who had lost her signals, since she flew none; but he admired whoever had built her and he doubted if he'd seen a fore-and-aft topsail rig so sweet in all his years at sea, and sweetly kept too. He pointed to fiery brass and blinding paint, reflecting the town dreaming in velvet on three sides of the bay.

Then Captain Begg smiled, for a flag ascended her mainmast just as the schooner swung girlishly, to reveal on her rounded stern the legend *Hope Dempsey*, Casablanca, painted in English and idiosyncratic but skilful Arabic.

And Captain Begg stood up, raising his glass.

Captain Horace Quelch had come back early to the islands, risking by a defiant week his amnesty, not due to begin until the first of November. It could be his last challenge, to show he had sold only his liberty to Laforgue the Pirate Chaser, never his spirit – and gambling that Count Estaban, the republic's governor, would turn a blind eye to a Cross of St George now standing straight as a Spaniard's spine at his topgallant.

'Here's to the last Christian pirate,' said Captain Begg and Don Victor was bound to join him in his toast.

Don Victor guessed that Count Estaban, a great diplomat, would choose to ignore Quelch's affront, rather than try to arrest the pirate and succeed only in chasing him back to open seas where, from Aden to Zarzamora, he could continue his clever and ruthless trade. For Quelch was the only pirate Laforgue had ever been forced to strike a bargain with.

Now, even as the muezzin began their exquisite calls to prayer from Las Cascadas's etiolated spires, the strains of a defiant gramophone came up to those who still took an interest in the schooner. A tune popular during and after the Great War of 1915, a guitar, an accordion and various oddly shaped rhythm-sticks, a Latin dance.

Captain Begg, yearning for Don Harold's glass, thought he saw against a porthole's oil-lit yellow the shadows of his old friends, Captain Quelch and Colonel Pyat, performing the tango with the grace everyone had so admired when, in their glory days, they had all been comradely adversaries on the routes between Alexandria and New Orleans.

Next morning, when he went down to the port to buy his bread and his *Al Païs*, Begg heard that Captain Quelch was only awaiting a passenger and would be leaving again on the afternoon tide. Whereupon Captain Begg, anxious not to miss this opportunity, hired a boatman in the harbour and was rowed out to the *Hope Dempsey*, to be greeted enthusiastically by Horace Quelch, who had last served with Begg on Albanian minesweepers during the War of the Balkan Succession.

'I hope I'm not disturbing you, old boy.' Begg embraced his old rival.

Horace Quelch kissed the navy man on both bearded cheeks. 'My dear Albert! I am forever *a vostro beneplacito* for you! What brings you to Don Estaban's little fiefdom?'

Captain Begg explained that he was on an official visit. He admired the ship. He marvelled at her smartness.

'I have the best crew in the world,' explained Quelch modestly.

The two old seadogs spent a comfortable couple of hours together in Quelch's bookish, almost fussy, cabin and caught up on mutual pals – pirates or King's Navy, it hardly mattered from their distance – and their successes, failures or resolutions of other sorts. Half a bottle of superb Armagnac was also consumed, together with four Castro cigars, to make the future look hopeful to them again and their past nothing lost, merely a confirmation that it was still satisfying and rewarding to steer a course that always had at least a few unexpected currents in it.

Thus rejuvenated, Captain Begg made it to his dinghy, with many further expressions of affection and declarations of the most profound comradeship, also faith in the years to come, and passed out, to be carried tenderly back to shore by one of Captain Quelch's own crew.

Albert Begg (now a Commander) would say: 'I never did see his passenger go aboard, though I found out later, of course, who it was.' He would offer as authority for his own report the fact that Quelch's passenger was a distant relative on his uncle's side.

In Which Captain Quelch's Expectations are Thoroughly Defeated but not Entirely Disappointed

Captain Quelch was deeply satisfied that society was about to repay its debt to him in the person of Count von Bek whose agent had offered half-a-million gold ryads for a comfortable passage with some small cargo to Essaouira which, in those days, was a port famous for the piety of its citizens and the briskness of its African arms trade. Knowing he could out-run anyone from Laforgue down, Quelch saw the job as an easy one. He felt his Kentish farm become reality when he accepted the offer, which would also be excellent cover for him to unload an embarrassing quantity of long boxes containing what had been in their day the best Martini repeating carbines ever smuggled to the Rif. 'Now you can get more per gun from some fat Casablanca merchant who wants one to hang over his marble mantel and lie about how he took it from a grateful legionnaire who had begged for and received his mercy at the Battle of Ouarzazate, than you once got for a whole case! It's easy money, old boy. But is it sporting? The profit's huge and nobody shoots you if the goods should prove faulty. *Caveat emptor*, indeed! It's a turning world, isn't it, my dear Count!'

He chatted man-to-man with his mysterious passenger who murmured responses from within a great weather-cloak but did not seem ready for conversation. Quelch displayed the interior of the luxurious little saloon and departed with almost religious courtesy as he accepted his first quarter-million in a velvet purse of intricate Berber ornament, and said that the count was welcome on the bridge whenever the count was so disposed; meanwhile the cargo luggage was being carefully stowed, as directed. After securing his gold, Quelch went to give particular attention to the usual collection of massive cabin trunks without which no German nobleman was able to travel a mile or two to an overnight ball, and a longer, narrower box, tightly wrapped in dark, blood-red cloth bound with long braids of glistening silver and gold, a baroque jewelled crucifix burning upon the upper surface.

Quelch judged this last to be a family relic, being brought under some archaic vow to a North African resting place, where an ancestor had once lost his heart to a local Fatima. Doubtless the count was that unfortunate relative chosen to supervise the digging up of the elderly romantic's corpse (no matter what its condition) as soon as the yearning ancestor's hated spouse was safely gone from this world to reconciliation in the next.

The fad for disinterment and exotic reburial had been popular for over fifty years and showed no sign of disappearing. Quelch put it all down to cheap yellowback novels by E Mayne Hull and Pierre Loti, not to mention those interminable Frances Day musical comedies, forever touring *The Desert Song* about the Levant and Magrib and still depressingly popular with German and British residents.

When the anchors were up and his exquisite schooner blossoming under full sail, flaunting all the laws of the sea, pushing hard towards Tripoli, his passenger appeared in the wheelhouse revealing herself as the famous adventuress Countess Rose von Bek, whereupon Captain Quelch dryly advised her to take the ship's boat and row like hell for Las Cascadas because his crew was as fine a bunch of hand-picked oriental nancy-boys as you could wish to find ashore or afloat.

'But they don't like women much. They reckon, my dear Countess, that women bring bad luck. They threw a pretty little thing of fourteen overboard only a month or two back. They have a strict code, don't you know, and take a firm moral line against anyone who transgresses it. Her boyfriend had a longer, more conspicuous and altogether grislier finish. A sore little bottom by the end of the day, what? Proper punishment for any naughty nipper. In their book, at any rate. And mine, really.'

The Rose ignored this teasing. She recognised Quelch's kind and had his measure, but she took the precaution of having the crew assembled for a few minutes. Addressing them in their own languages she informed them that they were fools intent on ensuring their destruction if they burdened their souls with superstition. They were drowning, she said, in their own shit, their own ignorance. They would never be free or fulfil their dreams unless they educated themselves and learned to behave as civilised men. Then she informed them that she was paying a large sum for her passage; thus, for the duration of her time aboard, she would be their commander.

The lascars looked once to Quelch, who turned his shrugging back on them; then they knelt as a man to offer her their hearts and their lives.

'Bad luck for whom, Horace?' she asked, sideways at him.

And he was bound to grin and tip his dirty cap to her. At which the Rose immediately fell under his charm, experiencing a powerful sensation, mixed lust and profound recognition. She had lost her heart to the old pirate. A tiny gasp escaped her perfect lips.

CHAPTER THREE

In Which a Famous Angel is Discussed

In the old days Quelch would always spend his Christmas break with Albert and Caroline Begg. It was Albert Begg who had given him a taste for the sea and helped him find the courage to trade places and professions with his twin brother, the salty Maurice.

While a guest at Sporting Club Square, Quelch would every evening accompany his host round the gardens. The square was at its best in the late autumn with its windows' yellow light softening the glowing terracotta touched by a setting orange sun. The great London trees were still red and golden brown, not yet in full fall, and beyond them were the stately silhouettes of those uniquely ordered buildings, each mansion block a different architectural conceit, a wedding cake in Buckingham brick, and then a pink aura, a light blue sky.

Once, stopping beside his favourite bed of late dahlias, Captain Begg had asked Quelch, then a rather timid housemaster, if he had ever heard of the Nation of Angels, a supernatural world in which ideal versions of ourselves wage war against evil? Quelch admitted that he had not. He only knew, he said, of one legendary angel, the Rose of Sporting Club Square herself, who was said to be a particular guardian of the Beggs.

Captain Begg had smiled at this. 'But one has to be a true innocent to see her, I'm told, so I've no chance and you neither, old chum.'

Ironically, in those days, Quelch really did have a chance, but his own romantic sensibilities had led him away from innocence until here he was, the most feared old swaggerer on either side of the Tideless Sea.

Now, as he admitted the extent of his fascination with the Rose, he recalled that legend vividly. He believed in his bones that the famous Angel was with him on board. What was worse he had fallen in love with her. But worse still, she was attracted to him. He was conquered. He was terrified.

For the first few otherwise agreeable days, while the schooner turned and steered on secret currents, moved by winds known only to Quelch and his crew, the Rose and Captain Quelch kept as wide a distance as possible as each wrestled with chaotic emotions. The third day, at dinner, they declared their madness and accepted it.

Contrary to the Captain's predictions, the crew became deeply sentimental and were moved by the union, celebrating it by giving extra pride to their duties and cheering the couple whenever they appeared together on deck. So the rest of the voyage was spent in a kind of ecstasy; with Essaouira reached, the rifles sold cheaply and carelessly and the countess's chief errand put in abeyance once she had delivered the cabin trunks (full of modern Mausers) to her partner 'Rabaq Bey. She then returned her attention to the enchanting Captain Quelch who wished to sail with her to his old stronghold and show her its beauty and his treasure.

CHAPTER FOUR

In Which Our Lovers are Roused from their Glamour by a Monstrous Manifestation

Castella de Las Piños: for years this Spanish-style fortified village, with its outrageously baroque Gaudi castle, had never fallen to an enemy gun and rarely seen so much as an enemy mast. The return of their popular chief and his bride was welcomed with considerable festivity by the citizens, some of whom had even served a season or two of their own with the Rose, when she had belonged to the Brotherhood of the Coast, called the Barbary Vixen by her enemies or the Red Angel by her admirers. Here was a fitting spouse for their captain; a goddess to adore. Her sword, Swift Thorn, she now sported on her hip and Quelch was both amused and besotted by her dash, her graceful choreography.

Barnaby Slyte, elected Mayor of Las Piños, offered the general sentiment when he spoke on the quayside and hoped the master and mistress had come to settle down for a while.

'That's for Fate to decide, good old Slyte,' says Captain Quelch, clapping his portly bo'sun on the back. 'But I have a feeling I'll be sticking my feet up for a while, at least.'

Then, with the townsfolk behind them, as colourful a mob of lace-trimmed butchers and their doxies as ever graced a pirate fortress, Quelch took her up the winding street to his Moorish gateway, rival to the Alhambra, and then into the castle, a filigree fantasy in

four-foot granite blocks and carved marble, to order the place empt-
ied so that he might take her privately to his vaults stacked with the
loot of three continents, enough to make Monte Cristo's wealth seem
modest. It had been accumulated, Quelch boasted, wholly through
ransoming fat daughters of the Tripoli Merchants, every one of
whom was returned to her father with her innocence intact.

'Still blood money, Horace,' she insisted, continuing an ongoing
argument. 'Earned by the employment of terror and force.'

'Well,' says Captain Quelch, 'true enough, my dear Rose, but it's a
complicated world and not every one of those charming little ladies
was pleased to be restored. I get their letters. To this day.' He bowed
to her, deeply, his back towards his mounds of treasure, and he
picked up a gorgeous Egyptian necklace, gold and turquoise and
rubies, offering it on the flat of his hand.

He was too much of a gentleman to show his disappointment when
she refused the gift. After all, he told himself, it was this prim quality
which he so admired in her. He blamed his public school education,
but he was helpless before its endless power.

Lost Pines, as the English called it, was famous for the tall ever-
greens which framed its elegant white domes and towers, as orderly
and neat a port as any on the Magribi coast. Her huge population of
cats kept the streets clean as the houses and the whole town was
touched by a pleasant scent of sage and rosemary.

As well as the Mausers, which had made her a good profit, even at
that low price, the Rose had also carried four kilos of Meng &
Ecker's Number 1 Special Mixture, which was currently banned in
Morocco, where the State had the monopoly, and thus worth a
fortune on the red market. She had been planning to move up the
coast to Tafouelt, the walled city of the Blue Men, and trade her
M&E with the Taureg for their silver and their ivory. An ounce or
two of this was broken out and placed in Horace Quelch's ornate
brass hookah, which dominated the centre of his leather-panelled
private smoking room, painted in the Persian mode and full of
luscious Leighton paintings and Crane tiles, part of the Lipton
salvage when the millionaire grocer's yacht was found abandoned
on Fever Sound in 1919.

The lovers shared their memories and elaborated upon each other's
dreams, aiming for a state of visual and spiritual consciousness
neither had experienced since their early days but which now seemed
achievable again. They were almost successful and the memory was
sweet reward enough. They indulged those elegiac tastes to which the
visionary romantic is prone, when denied melodrama or at very least

a doomed love affair, and they wept once or twice for a lost idyll, but mostly they remembered their age and station and kept enough humour in reserve to remind them that this was almost certainly no more than a pleasant lull in a lifetime of exotic action.

Sure enough, after a couple of weeks, the couple was aroused from some intricately comfortable embrace by the news that the *Hope Dempsey* was missing from the harbour, her crew with her. Could it be that Quelch's hand-picked homophiles had betrayed him, after all?

The Rose, sickened by this sudden return of common sense, raised an exquisite hand to her perfect lips and spoke in an appalled whisper. 'Oh, no! The cargo!'

'Just your mysterious box, Countess.' Her lover was unmoved by his vessel's high value but knew that a hull as clean and responsive as that only came under your feet once in a lifetime. He was determined to pursue and recapture his beloved schooner.

The Rose was quickly persuaded of her own self-interest and together they called for a crew from amongst the townsfolk, to take the cumbersome old ocean-going dhow, *Shahrazad*, in pursuit of the stolen schooner.

CHAPTER FIVE

In Which The Rose Reveals Something About an Undying Ancestor

Their eager, if rusty, complement gradually remembered how to coax the best out of a sluggish vessel, and the *Shahrazad* was soon making good speed through the outlying islands, the course of the *Hope Dempsey* reported from watch-towers set up to warn of unfamiliar ships in the pirate domain.

The Rose and Captain Quelch studied maps in the charthouse. They found the course a little baffling. 'Why should they be setting into the Cameroon Bite, a place avoided by even the most daring pilots and sporting sailors?' asks Quelch, taking a tidy measurement.

'Because they no longer care if they live or die,' the Rose told him. 'They serve another master now.'

'What more do you know?' he demanded, laying down his rule.

'Only that there is something alive in your hold, Captain.'

'An animal?'

'If you like. I would describe it as a creature which has lost all reason, all humanity, yet which was once everything a man might wish to be.'

'You mean you had a living *man* in that box you brought aboard, Rose?'

'Not living in any sense you mean, Horace. This poor monster is cursed with longevity, yet can never know happiness. For centuries he has wandered the world, desperate for death, seeking, he says, the one human being who can save him and bring him rest. I have listened to him, dreaming within his prison – a prison his relatives constructed for him, enjoining me to grant him the peace he sought. Oh, make no mistake, Horace, he is active and very powerful – able to put a score of people under his spell at once. He has profound knowledge of every oriental and occidental science. He recognises no morality in the ordinary meaning of the term. He is fearless because he has feared everything and been destroyed by nothing. He exists only to feed his bizarre cravings and is utterly without compassion. He is dedicated I believe to destroying what little order this civilisation of ours had tried to erect against Chaos and Old Night. I was told he would remain dormant for at least six months, long enough to do what I had to do. He has gathered power, even as he slept! I feared as much, but I quieted myself, indulged myself.'

'But what does this mean, my dear?' he wished to know.

'It means, Horace, that we have a monster loose amongst us. I was entrusted with the mission of taking him to the far Sahara and burying him at the abandoned Oasis of the Ouled Näil, which was poisoned with radium and is now avoided by nomads and caravans alike. You are not bound to help me recapture the creature, Horace. This is a task for which I should be entirely responsible.'

But Quelch was resolute. 'He has my ship, Rose, my dear. And my crew? Don't you think he's put some sort of 'fluence on those obedient lascars? A monster indeed! You must tell me more of his story when it's politic. Meanwhile, I was equally lax and am equally bound to aid you in this matter.'

The Rose admitted that she could think of no better ally in such an enterprise. They smoked what remained of their M&E then retired to their bunk to await some revelation.

'He was known as Manfred, Count of Crete and Lebanon. He married a great-grandmother of the von Beks. There was no issue.'

'So he is not even a blood relative!' said Quelch.

[14]

'Many people believe him to be Jewish,' she said, 'though he denies this vehemently . . .'

'But that's a well-known story,' said Quelch, slowly, savouring his recollections. 'Browning did a poem on the subject. And so did Austin. My favourite's always Wheldrake. I knew him before the War, when he was living in Putney. He'd walk across the bridge at the same time that I was going out. I was in digs there, in one of those old rooming houses overlooking the Thames, all massive buttresses and gothic turrets, with rowing sheds on either side. Mrs Ottoman ran it and also served teas on her terrace during the summer, for the boating parties and oarsmen who made Ottoman's the favourite stopping place below Hammersmith and one of the most popular on the entire river, from Oxford to Greenwich. Wheldrake went there out of season, breaking his walk to enjoy a half-pint of beer before returning home to The Cedars. It was there that he signed my copy of *Bernice Beati* for me – before the police seized pretty much the whole edition from his printers. I became something of a protégé of his, I suppose. I used to be proud of that, but fashions change, don't they? *Cave quid dicis, quando, et cui*, eh? My mistake was always to be too outspoken. My patron became unfashionable, my own literary career was nipped in the bud and I was forced to take a job as housemaster at an obscure school on the Kent coast where I was forever plagued by fat boys, practical jokers and pious young heroes who, thank God, were mostly wiped out at the Battle of Buchenwald. Wasn't the Count of Crete mixed up with some scandal during the Second Empire? Some terrible financial thing in which thousands of ordinary people were ruined?'

'Who wasn't?' She had hardly listened to his anecdote.

'But why would he be taking my ship to the Cameroon Bite and how has he seduced my lascars? Their sense of self-preservation is their greatest virtue.'

'You could say the same about Count Manfred,' she murmured and then was unwilling to continue the conversation.

In Which Captain Albert Begg Finds Himself Once Again Involved with His Old Friend

Albert Begg was on his way back to Gibraltar when he received the news over the Morse that the *Hope Dempsey* had broken her parole and was heaving into forbidden waters, some kind of Arab craft pursuing her – both ships steering a bafflingly irregular course.

Captain Begg had orders to make for waters off the Cameroon Bite and observe the movements of the vessels, reporting back to Georgetown at regular intervals.

'This was familiar stuff,' Begg would tell his future listeners, 'since most of my service life was in Naval Intelligence, which is a wonderful niche for a chap who loves languages and has a passion for fiction. A comfortable berth in my time and probably still is – though you miss being able to tune in the Savoy Orpheans on the radio. Moreover my curiosity was whetted by my old friend's mysterious behaviour. I had it in mind to be of help to him, if that were possible within the broad terms of what we perceived (in that idiosyncratic arm of our service) as our duty.

'Needless to say,' (Begg continued), 'I was not going to expose either my ship or my crew to danger and had no intention of venturing into the Bite itself. The Rose, brave as she is, has only sailed into the Biloxi Fault, never through the Lavender Haze. I had no special qualities as a sailor and, as an observer, was not expected to do anything but let the second officer run things. My job was to study the movements of a pirate on broken parole but not to engage him. If in danger I should have the presence of mind to signal for help in good time. We had a nine-inch Bofors and an old Gatling for armament, sufficient for a fighting chance against a Zeppelin or a heavily armed fishing boat, but useless against modern aircraft. Still, we weren't likely to encounter anything very sophisticated – not that a gun would be proof against – so we ran up the usual signals and laid off below that appalling horizon . . .'

But such terrors were all in the past, of course, the Commander hastened to warn those listeners who were small children and beginning to look alarmed. Albert Begg realised it was as if someone had told him, when he was their age, that King Kong was still abroad and might come round the corner at any moment, walking down Olympia Avenue to tear the roof off the building and pluck them out like toy soldiers. 'No more a threat than old King Kong,' he said, to reassure them.

At this, the children became baffled. King Kong was no longer part of their mythology. Even the wild realities of thirty years ago seemed a little too fanciful for present tastes.

'Such uncertainties are abolished now and good riddance to them, I say. I am ready to enjoy the security and predictability achieved under this current triumph of Law and hang the obvious consequences. But you should study a little, my children, the experience of the past, because already in my short lifetime I see the same kind of people making the same mistakes, resulting in the same awful consequences for society at large. Avoid prescriptive politics, my dears, at all costs. They are un-English, whether they come from Left or Right. They are always wrong, always bad. And those who provide the prescriptions all too rarely suffer the consequences of their outrageous, egotistical follies. And there is nothing more time-wasting than a clash of prescriptions in parliament. It is the business of parliament to interpret the popular will, not patronise its voters!'

Whereupon he stopped himself and offered the children a grave apology. Turning to the adults he suggested, through some harmless code, he make a pretty little ending for the children and tell the true tale later. The parents agreed to this, so he obliged.

The children were treated to a tale of monsters vanquished and were sent to bed, bearing with them that comfortable thrill of a demon confronted and overpowered. But their parents rejoined in Begg's sitting room and made themselves more comfortable by the fire with full glasses, their attention upon the old salt, who never failed to enjoy the effects of his own retailings, but he avoided any further political excursions.

'The sky,' (he went on), 'was alive with sinuous funnels of gas – browns and blacks and greys – through which a hellish sun burned murky rays and the sea was agitated, neurotic. There was no soothing rhythm to the waters of the Cameroon Bite. You have seen the pictures, I am sure, but you could never imagine the experience of being there, even at so great a distance.

'We had recently had our optics renewed and could get some pretty good sightings. Soon we had made out the *Hope Dempsey* under full sail, steering an irregular but rapid course that was roughly north-west. Behind her, making impressive speed, came an ordinary trading dhow, by some means following almost exactly in the schooner's wake.

'The mystery was that the Lavender Haze lay off to their starboard and their course lay away from it. So they were not, after all, planning to enter the Haze. And what of the vampire – or whatever it was – which now commanded the *Hope Dempsey*? But I race ahead of my tale . . .

'Two days later, pretty much due north of the Haze, when the ships had disappeared from view and not been sighted by us for twenty-four hours, we picked up the outlines of a small cock boat, its canvas in rags, making desperate speed, by another queer route, towards us.

'I gave the order to shorten the distance between us.

'I had a feeling we were picking up survivors.'

CHAPTER SEVEN

In the Shadow of the Haze

'I really wasn't prepared for anything radical,' said the Rose, handing Quelch's spyglass back to him.

'There's always a price to pay for these idylls, in my experience,' Quelch told her. 'It's in the nature of our game, dear Rose. But I must admit I expected a more natural conclusion to our affair. I suppose this way is at least dramatic. Good theatre, perhaps, but hard on old bones.'

'I've never known a sailor more stuffed with superstitions and discredited opinion,' she said. 'You can make a game of this, Horace, as much as you wish. But if we do not find Count Manfred, there will be the most catastrophic consequences, not least for my father and the entire Lombardian government!'

Impressed by her tone, Quelch assured her that it was not important whether he took her seriously – though indeed the case did seem serious – since he would soon have the wheel of the *Hope Dempsey* firmly under his two hands, her crew disciplined and about their ordinary business and everything ship-shape, as it was when they first anchored in Lost Pines Bay. 'It's in my self-interest, Rose.'

The Rose accepted this for the time being, knowing that her lover was not a thorough-going exponent of enlightened self-interest. The ex-pirate was bearing it in mind to learn more of that valuable box and its wormy occupant. He knew that people had killed to get it. What kind of creature was capable of controlling his lascars from within a coffin? If he could find out more he knew that such information might bring a handsome profit from the Romans, the Greeks or any other friendly government wanting to be privy to Lombardy's particular secrets.

'Our first task is to engage them,' she reminded him, 'and there is still too much distance between us.'

Then she proposed a plan whereby she took the wheel and used a skill or two of her own.

To his credit Quelch had every faith in her and congratulated her when her superior navigation got them a mile or two closer to the wandering *Hope Dempsey*. And then he understood their course.

'Only one island remained above water after the upheaval,' he said. 'It's known as Duke's Island by the English and Isla de Juifes by the Portuguese and Arcadians. It's said to conceal a vast treasure buried since the time of Christ (by Joseph of Arimathea) and it has an underground castle ruled by an undying lord mourning the loss of his abducted daughter and hating all living creatures as much as he hated himself! Could your Count Manfred have left Duke's Island and now be returning?'

'If that were the case and this journey at his instigation,' declared the Rose, 'then why should I have been charged with the task of burying him in that radium dump at Oasis Ouled Näil? No, Captain Quelch, it is my ancestor's happy adaptability, his desire to refuse the fact of death at any price, which motivates this voyage. I would swear to it. He knows so much. I am not at all sure who or what he will find at the Isla de Juifes! But I do not think it will be himself.'

She looked away towards the gathering coils and gassy knots which passed, faint shadows, within the icy depths of the Lavender Haze. She felt almost defeated.

CHAPTER EIGHT

Addressing the Jungle

'These days,' Begg continued, 'it is impossible to understand the terror in which the Haze was held. It had appeared overnight and while no ship that had sailed into it had ever returned, occasionally it spewed something out which had no business breathing ordinary mortal air and moving beneath an ordinary mortal sun. The thing had spawned an entire industry in almanacs and geomancies, not to mention religious and scientific cults.

'We still have some of those cults hanging on in spite of all their evidence having been banished to whatever part of the astral plane it originally sprang from. My only regret was that the cults were not sent back to limbo with the object of their faith. But you can imagine the awful fear of the Haze which must have filled the Rose and Captain Quelch, for all their wide experience of the world. Only madness and agony lay within. And death of course.'

He explained how, by combining their considerable sailing skills, they managed to steer the lumbering *Shahrazad* into the little hidden harbour of Duke's Island and find the *Hope Dempsey*, an affronted aristocrat but none the worse for her experience, recently abandoned, her crew deep in a sleep that looked sorcerous while the oblong box from the hold lay with its lid torn off and a swathe of red cloth draped over ropes of gold and silver hiding a jewelled crucifix, perhaps some sort of device adopted by the occupant as a means of identification. Its meaning puzzled Captain Quelch. Was this a secret of the Lombardian royal family's? Only an aristocrat would abandon such a valuable piece without a thought. He made no move towards it but followed the Rose to the main deck.

'There,' she said, 'you have your ship and your crew again, Captain, and none the worse for wear, I'd guess. As soon as those boys wake up they'll be ready to follow you to hell and back, mark my words. You can sail on now. Only leave me the dhow, the box and a couple of your lascars, so I can get away from here when my duty is done.'

'Well, madam,' says Quelch after a little thought, 'my curiosity has me now and won't let me go until it's satisfied. I'd be obliged if you'd let me join your expedition to the interior. I could be of help. I am something of an expert with the revolver.' And privately he considered the potential political import of whatever secret the old count carried and which could so embarrass Rose von Bek's Irish father, the engineer O'Bean, or cause trepidation in the House of Lombardy.

Touched, but not entirely convinced, the Rose accepted his help. After taking refreshment aboard the schooner, they headed a small expedition up into the jungle while Bo'sun Slyte, sweat running like mountain rivers down the soft geography of his upper body, took charge of the hands and gave orders to revive the lascars, if that were possible.

Barnaby Slyte waited four days before he allowed himself to suspect that his captain and the rest weren't returning. Only now were the lascars beginning to awake and they spoke sluggishly in pidgin about a 'berry bad, berry, berry bad debil fella belong deepdown nogood'. But they could offer no further description of the sea-thief who had commanded them from a rope-bound coffin deep within the hold.

All that Slyte learned, Begg said, increased his sense that his master and mistress were leading their men against some creature of demonic malice, whose psychic powers were impossibly advanced.

Meanwhile, Barnaby Slyte was confounded. He feared it was his duty to lead an expedition up the trail through the jungle to the castle, to learn of his captain's fate.

He was not to know that Quelch's messenger, a distant cousin, had been bitten by a cobra and collapsed on the road, which the natives called the Sacred Trail of Death and which they travelled only when their time had come.

CHAPTER NINE

A Confusion of Wanderers

Protected by local superstition, Quelch, the Rose and their party reached the top of the wooded hill without serious incident and stood beside a deep moat staring up at a massive Gothic castle, evidently of late-Victorian or even Edwardian restoration, combining modern comfort with archaic grandeur. Captain Quelch noted the excellent pointing.

'Rather reassuring.' He gave his attention to the cylinders of his twin Colts, rubbing the barrels on his sleeve to shine them up a bit. He replaced the pistols in his belt. 'Are we ready, Countess?'

The Rose drew her slender sword, Swift Thorn, and led the way across the unguarded drawbridge into the castle's barbican which had none of the depressing Norman severity on which it was modelled but had been laid out in a series of geometric flower-beds, full of every variety of seasonal blooms and shrubs. There was a settled, domestic air to the place, even though it was deserted.

Receiving no response to their echoing halloos, they entered the door of the main keep. The interior was cheerful and well lighted and the papered walls showed a preference for William Morris and the arts and crafts movement, particularly the Scottish school. Captain Quelch recognised many original paintings which he had thought lost.

At length they entered a warm, book-lined, oak-beamed hall, twinkling with polished brass and copper, in which a hearty fire blazed. The furniture was largely Eastlake, of a somewhat heavy ecclesiastical style, perfectly in tune with the revived romanticism of the castle. Wine, spirits and beer were arranged on the hospitable sideboards. Two massive leather easy chairs stood either side of the fire and on an elbow table next to one sat a book (*Don Estaban and Duke Rupoldo* by Carlisle), an empty glass and a jar of mints; there was a footstool before this chair, the indentations showing that it had been recently used. The farthest walls were lined with glass-fronted bookshelves containing a conspicuous array of disparate bindings and titles, representing all periods and types of human literature.

'The home of a retired gentleman, I would say,' murmured Captain Quelch. But he kept his hand on a pistol.

'And, it seems, a serious recluse,' the Rose added.

Whereupon, as if summoned by their references, suddenly a side door opened with a startling creak and from behind it emerged a gaunt, uncouth figure, its stooped shadow flung upon the books as it extended an unappealing hand to Quelch and announced that it was Count Manfred, Lord of Castle Zion, and that the travellers were welcome to rest and take refreshment but that they were trespassing and should be aware that they were disturbing one who did not relish human company.

This statement was belied by the happy security and hospitable air of the place, but the pirates said nothing. The hands looked to the sideboard and at Count Manfred's signal helped themselves to drinks. The count regretted that his servants were at present visiting the mainland but they would be back at any time. Meanwhile he would be grateful if they respected his need for privacy. 'I am a scholar, used to my own company.' He spoke in a resonant, gloomy voice which seemed a little cracked at the edges, as if it had been used too much or too little.

The Rose, however, was impatient with this charade, for she recognised her errant relative. 'This is simply not your style, Count Manfred. Why dress in rags and tatters and pay such poor attention to personal appearance when this furniture is so lovingly kept? This is a room of a sybarite. You were never that! I suspect that you have no right to be here. I know you for my ancestor, whom I am charged to bury at the Oasis of the Ouled Näil. I beg you, for all our sakes, to end your play-acting, for it is dreadfully unconvincing, and come with me to your long-deserved rest.'

At this the creature drew himself up, the deep hollows of his eye-sockets blazing with angry fires, and his long-fingered, shaking hands went to his head as if to protect it from further assault. 'Rest?' cried the monster. 'Rest?' His laughter was hollow. 'In the radium pits? Oh, I have begged for rest so many times! I have yearned for release from this terrible enslavement of life. I have climbed to the peaks of the world's tallest mountains, flung myself into the deepest gorges, given myself up to the wildest torrents, descended into the maelstrom and sunk into the bubbling lava of that same Vesuvius that destroyed my Pompeii town-house. Yet all to no avail. Death has been denied me. Rest is unattainable – or seemed so until now. Rest, Rose von Bek, has eluded me for almost two thousand years! I grew reconciled that I was never to know it. I long to be buried in my native soil with the full rites of the church and a tranquil soul reunited with its redeemer in Heaven. I do not deserve some desert pit, where I am never fully dead but consigned to spend eternity amongst the poisons and residues Society would rather forget it ever created! Is that justice? All I ask is for a true end to this. I have to go back to Nuremberg. Blood calls to blood. It is one of our most basic under-standings. I am tired of my struggle. I need to go home! *Mein Kampf! Mein Kampf!* Is it over at last?'

Captain Quelch showed evident impatience with this self-dramatising rhetoric. 'What did you do to my crew, Count Manfred?' he demanded. 'What unnatural power did you exert over them to make them bring you here?'

'Power?' The Count of Crete threw back his cadaverous head, cackling his mockery. 'Power? What? Am I the Devil? No, I am as human as you, Captain Quelch. The power I had was the power of their stupid, superstitious minds. Nothing else. I have no special supernatural skills. One of your boys was curious and tried to open the box. Happily I am possessed of considerable physical strength. I was grateful for my freedom. When they saw me appear on deck the lascars thought Death commanded them. I told them I would take them with me into the Land of Shadows unless they worked hard and got the ship to this island in record time. It is not always visible.

'Very little energy was required to bend those lascars to my will. It never requires much energy. My appearance and their fear achieves most of what I need. They were terrified that if they slept I would suck their brains and souls out, so they made liberal use of the cocaine each of them had been planning to smuggle into Barcelona.

'As a result, when they got to this island they were thoroughly crazed and absolutely exhausted, falling asleep on their feet. I had grown attached to one or two of them, but I left them all on the schooner, then made my way up here. To my castle.' This last was said with a certain defiance.

'It's plain to us that you neither prepared this fire nor laid down that book, sir,' said the Rose. 'This castle is not your work.'

He turned aside with a slouching, surly motion of his shoulders. He stared into the fire. 'What's that to you, madam? My servants are responsible for this. Now, leave me in peace. Or stay the night, if you wish. But do not expect me to accompany you to the radium cemetery. I intend to return to Hamburg and from there make my way slowly east. I have some old debts to repay. For almost two thousand years I have wandered and I have grown weary. Now, here, I can find honest death . . .'

'Good Heavens, old boy! You're not . . .' Quelch found it almost impossible to utter the words, 'suggesting that you are the original Wandering Jew?'

At this the count drew himself up, his entire horrid frame trembling with deep emotion. He moved his head until his cold eyes glared with something akin to passion into Quelch's own.

'What?' he demanded. 'Wandering *what*? You braying fool! You short-lived ape. You make the same obtuse assumptions as all the others!' His pitted features twisted in torment and anger. 'Cretin! I have travelled the world for forty lifetimes and more, seeking the one human soul who could save me – or one human being who would believe my story. Almost two thousand years and I never discovered that one creature. Not one in all the centuries of my agony. None, that is – *until now*!'

'There's no excuse for bad manners, old boy,' remonstrated Quelch mildly.

The other pirates looked embarrassed, as if they were regretting leaving the harbour. One of them murmured that he was ready to believe anything after the events of the past few days but feeling the count's eye upon him spoke up nervously. 'And what is that story, sir?'

The creature's hollow sockets burned with recollected agonies and disappointments. 'It is a tragic one,' he replied. 'A tale of terrible events and unjust adventure. I was born on the site of modern Nuremberg, the spiritual capital of the Teutonic people. My name is not Lazarus but Manfred and I am not Jewish. True, it is impossible to kill me or for me to kill myself. True I am doomed to live forever, for failing to give Christ a cup of water on his way to Calvary, but the whole thing was a dreadful mistake. I was employed as an agent for a Greek grain dealer and just happened to be in Jerusalem on the day. I had no direct involvement with any of the proceedings. I was never guilty. Can you not see why I am so obsessed with a sense of injustice? I have endured every kind of insult, every calumny! And much of it because of mistaken identity. No, my friends, it is not the Wandering Jew who stands before you . . .'

He paused, staring again into the fire as if he saw the flames of Hell there and yearned for them. 'I am Manfred the Goth. And I am the Wandering Gentile.'

At this Captain Quelch looked sceptical and even the most gullible pirates were unimpressed. It was left for the Rose to ask the obvious: 'Are you suggesting that for all this time the world has been mistaken and that there is no such person as the Wandering Jew?'

He turned on her again, his bony fingers stroking his body as if seeking wounds. 'Did I tell you that? Oh, the Wandering Jew exists. He is very much alive. For almost two thousand years I have pursued him, following rumours, myth, folk-tales – I have walked the length and breadth of all the world's continents. I have seen miraculous sights and had thousands of extraordinary experiences. I knew he existed. I believed that as soon as I found him, and if that meeting were witnessed, then I would know rest. I would be freed from the curse and the world would see at last how specifically I had suffered. Almost two millennia – and I never discovered him and was never redeemed. How I begged the God above to release me from my bondage, to bring us together so that the curse would be lifted. All I had to do was prove to another human soul that I was cursed as he was cursed. Then the soul of the Wandering Gentile would be at peace. Now it has come about. My soul can return to the womb of its fatherland, in Nuremberg. I shall go first to Hamburg and travel a little in Bohemia and Poland, concluding my journey in Warsaw perhaps. The route will to a large degree define itself. But I shall die where I was born. It is all I ask.'

'I wish you luck, old boy.' Captain Quelch was uncomfortable and not sure why. 'Well, where's the original occupant of this place, then? You haven't murdered the poor chap, I hope.'

The cadaverous wretch again glared, uttering cryptic curses and spitting out his words in a disgusted stream. '*Poor chap*, is it? *Poor chap*, eh? Bah! Save your sympathy for me, my dear sir, not for that *poor chap*! Ugh! Imagine my chagrin when I arrived here only a few hours since and was not challenged. I knew a kind of elation. It was as if I would soon meet my twin soul. I had imagined him suffering as I had suffered, trying to kill himself, standing upon the peaks of midnight mountains in the Himalayas yelling his torment to the skies. I have wandered so painfully, so hopelessly, so needlessly. Have you any notion of what my eyes beheld when I entered this room? Can you imagine the filthy cosiness of the whole sickening scene? I saw him as soon as I opened the door, but he did not at first see me.

'There he sat, in that chair, oblivious to everything but his reading. He lazed in a comfortable smoking jacket, holding a letter from a loved one, his feet on the footstool in front of a blazing fire which sent cheerful shadows round the room, merry as Christmas, beside him on his table a glass of brandy, an opened book, a jar of mints, while the cabinet gramophone you see over there played exquisite Alkan. Could anyone have witnessed such obscenity and not act as I acted? Remember, Captain Quelch, I sought the fellow out for almost two thousand years! I imagined him doing as I did – tramping the solitary trails and rocky roads of an unjust world, forever doomed to seek forgiveness, a fellow sufferer.'

'Are you saying that the rightful occupant of this castle actually is the Wandering Jew?' the Rose exclaimed with sudden understanding.

Her relative seemed to approve of her intelligence.

His cold eyes lit with something akin to pleasure. 'Exactly!' he said. '*His* name is Lazarus not mine! *He* refused Christ a cup of water! *He* is the true carrier of this curse, not I!'

'What have you done with him?' the Rose wished to know, but the count dismissed her question with an impatient gesture.

'The creature confessed all this to me not an hour ago! He has been sitting in more or less the same spot, in more or less the same chair, at more or less the same time of day, since the ninth century! He has not

[26]

wandered at all! He has known nothing but comfort and good will, the respect and love of his children, grandchildren, great-grandchildren and so on. I demanded to be told how he had suffered and he admitted that he thought he had suffered once, but the suffering was a mere faded memory. It was at about the time of the Diet of Worms, he said, that it occurred to him there was precious little point in wandering, when all common sense suggested taking advantage of the situation and settling down comfortably somewhere to enjoy life as it came. Over the course of centuries his sensible investments made him immensely rich. He married a succession of mortal wives and all his offspring did well in various humanitarian vocations and almost invariably left the world a better place . . .

'The Jew lived in luxury and security on this island,' Count Manfred continued. 'During all those hundreds of years in which I sought him so painfully, he was sedately settled with his books, his companion, his children, protected by the superstitious fear of all sailors who gave his home waters wide berth, refusing to accept that the Isla de Juifes even existed. Occasionally, he told me, he would rescue some shipwrecked maiden who had been ill-used by men and found his patient good humour a welcome change.

'The boys, he told me, he usually slaughtered. He said their blood was particularly efficacious in the preparation of alchemical potions. He was mocking me, of course. He admitted his lies later when, under my close attentions, he became a little more eager to offer me the whole story . . . All his nasty little secrets came out in the end. Not such a gay duck, now, Sir Lazarus, eh?'

The Wandering Gentile uttered a chilling laugh, relishing his moment. Then he strode to a tall armoire, all oak and brass, and reached a claw-like hand for the door.

'He is in here now. You may have what's left of him, and welcome . . .'

CHAPTER TEN

A Mystery Solved –
and Another Begun!

And with that (continued Commander Begg) the Count of Crete
swept open the door!

After a little hesitation, out staggered a blinking, barefooted old
fellow of mild, healthy appearance, who shivered when he saw the
Wandering Gentile posturing before him and would not advance
further into his room until Manfred had sworn on his honour, and
what was left of his putrefying soul, that he would never again use a
feather on Herr Lazarus's soles.

'He is a devil!' declared Herr Lazarus. 'You have my eternal thanks
for this rescue.' He was small, plump, neatly bearded.

'Why was he torturing you?' asked Quelch. 'Does he seek your
treasure?'

'Treasure? My "treasure" isn't liquid. These days it is mostly tied
up in land. No, he wanted to know my eldest daughter's name. I told
him. We've always inspired writers, our family. Still he wouldn't
believe that it was indeed the same Rebecca who starred in *Ivanhoe*,
the novel. It's my genes. She had a little of my original blood, you see,
and went a good seven hundred years before the wrinkles started
showing, then she came to live with me. Her gravestone's in the back
garden. We were all fond of her. Sometimes I have half-a-dozen
relatives staying here. I'm never lonely.'

At this last remark the Wandering Gentile uttered a blood-chilling
growl and advanced as if to fix his rotting fingers about the throat of
the Wandering Jew, who frowned unhappily and stepped back a
little.

Several of the pirates, none in his first youth, tried to restrain
Count Manfred, but he was far too strong for them. He flung them
off, yet did not advance further on Herr Lazarus. Instead he leaned
forward, pointing an accusing forefinger. 'You old boaster! You com-
placent dolt! What right had you to discover reconciliation, even of
this earthly kind? What right, when I wandered round and round the
globe in search of you, only missing this island by a few miles because
I had been told it did not really exist and that no ship had ever
sighted it! But now, thanks to the Haze, you are exposed!

'Wretch! You deceived the world so cleverly. You cunningly made use of our honest credulity! How handsomely you profited from our simple Teutonic generosity. Do you know how many times I have circumnavigated this miserable little planet? How many storms I have weathered? How many times I have been swallowed by earthquakes, endured pestilences, pogroms, dungeons? I have been engulfed by volcanic lava at least fifteen times. I have been pursued and attacked through a thousand different wars. I have been hunted by mobs, by angry fathers and husbands, vindictive wives, crazed bed-fellows! I have known no mother's comfort. I have never enjoyed the confidence or advice of a father. I have tasted blood so many, many times – yet have never seen my own long enough for a drop of it to fall upon the ground! Oh, you do not deserve such peace of mind! What a deep injustice is this! How have you earned such rest?'

The Wandering Jew was pouring fresh drinks for his guests. He crossed the Turkish carpet to place a tumbler of brandy in his tormentor's palpitating hand. 'I sat down and thought it all out one day,' he said reasonably. 'There were, after all, a lot worse fates that could befall a Jew than being cursed with eternal life. I decided to go, as they say, with the flow. And here I am. About as contented and comfortable an immortal, I must admit, as any I've heard about! Why blame me? I simply made the best of things.'

Later the Rose told Begg how the wholesome old man exuded a sense of considerable peace and good will and was clearly content with his lot. She asked him if he did not regret the chance to die. Some would think he was being denied the promise of heaven. Of grace. He disagreed. 'This is heaven enough for me,' he said.

Again this produced a dramatic response in his rival who lifted up his long pale head and howled.

'Poor devil,' interjected Captain Quelch, trying to bring down the emotional temperature a little. 'Couldn't you both let bygones be bygones and work together? *Che sera sera*, as the Lombardians have it. Why not shake hands and call it a day? After all, at least one of you can now find his final resting place . . .' and he looked expectantly at the Wandering Gentile.

He was affronted. 'Why address *me* first?' the Gentile wanted to know. 'Why not that miserable hypocrite who, in a manner typical of his horrid race, has made himself comfortable in circumstances where it was not intended for him to be comfortable!' But he spoke hopelessly, in the tone of one long used to prejudice and rejection.

'Because Captain Quelch understands,' said the Jew patiently to the ensemble at large, 'that I am in no great hurry to wander anywhere. I am not in torment. I do not long for death et cetera, et cetera. In fact I have found, as far as I know, a perfectly adequate resting place and plan to remain here until the last Judgement. Not a bad spot to wait out eternity, all in all.'

'Tcha!' Again the Wandering Gentile was barely able to contain his fury. He appealed to the company. 'Look at these poor ruined feet of mine! Look at these wretched hands! Look at this torn flesh, this rotting body, these pathetic remains − these rags of clothing − these shreds of skin and shards of bone − these hideous scars! What an ugly creature I have become. Is it any wonder I am avoided, reviled, stoned, driven from the settlements of my fellows, never to know decent human company, placed in a box by my relatives who now seek to dump me in a radium pit! Why should I not hate you, who sits in contentment in your cosy home, drinking Twinings Assam and Ovaltine while wearing cardigans knitted for you by doting descendants?'

The Wandering Jew considered this, then answered reasonably. 'My dear sir − you, too, could have enjoyed pretty much the same life as mine. You did not *have* to wander, any more than I. You could have found yourself a little island, perhaps in the Hebrides or in the Indian Ocean, depending upon your taste in climate and so on, invested in a few long-term portfolios to pay for your needs and retired. In your own home you could be at very least decently fed and clothed, and you would not have to endure any insults. None.'

'He has a point, old boy,' says Captain Quelch. 'You seem to be complaining mostly that it was the Jew's idea to make the best of things and not yours. You were simply obsessed with finding him. It seems to me you've wasted your opportunities.'

Even the Rose thought this a little insensitive of him in the circumstances and it did seem to be the last straw, for the Wandering Gentile flung his brandy glass into the fireplace and let out an enormous roar of frustration and misery. 'Oh, damn him forever! Damn him to the deepest pit, the hottest hell!' he cried, gesticulating vigorously with his unnaturally long arms. 'I put my own curse upon you, Lazarus. Even when the Last Trump is sounded − *you shall never know death!*'

And with these thrilling words, which left ice in every heart, Manfred, Count of Crete, stormed from the room and was not seen there again. He made his way down the Sacred Trail of Death to the harbour where he was at first mistaken for the long-awaited messenger by Barnaby Slyte, who greeted him warmly and gratefully until the count entered a pool of silver moonlight and stood glaring up at him from the lower deck.

Which was how, said Commander Begg, the *Shahrazad* came so quickly to be abandoned by the pirates, enabling Count Manfred to take the boat under his own control, aided by two quaking lascars, who had the misfortune to be sharing the bunks of friends aboard.

Almost immediately one of the lascars escaped in the ship's cock boat and that was how he came eventually to be picked up by me. But I had only a partial story and was not to know the whole truth until much later.

Upon the lascar's urgent instruction I gave the order to pursue the *Shahrazad*, believing that she carried as prisoners Captain Quelch and the Rose . . .

It was a dramatic chase, through heavy seas, with winter coming out of Russia like a cat out of a dog's home – blind, ferocious and careless of anything that gets in its way – but just off Bilbao we caught up with her and put a shot across her, though she was virtually out of our jurisdiction. She hove to and I took a boarding party over.

The long and the short of it was, we found nothing suspicious about the dhow – no arms, contraband or prisoners. I had been deceived by the lascar or misinformed. It emerged that he had been referring to a different ship altogether. There was certainly nothing we could nail her captain for, unless it was his smell and general appearance which suggested that he was no great enthusiast for bathing. He was a tall, cadaverous individual with a bad head cold who held a heavily scented rag in front of his face most of the time. He had a strong foreign accent which I guessed to be Middle European.

The only thing that was remotely odd about the dhow was in the hold – a long, narrow box roughly wrapped in red velvet. When we opened it we found only some gold and silver cord and a beautiful crucifix which the captain said was all he had left of his family and, he guessed, perhaps his religion, too. It was the badge of a Papal emissary.

There was nothing for it but to share a glass of rum with the captain, who gave his name as Manfred, and let him explain how he had followed Captain Quelch to the Isla de Juifes, which he passed regularly, and had made sure his fellow captain was safely anchored before continuing on his way to Hamburg, where Manfred had some business. He had no idea, he said, why Quelch had decided to visit that jungly rock and suggested I ask him myself.

The old boy's story could not be contradicted, so we decided to escort him on his way for a bit, send in a report and let the matter drop, at least until we knew more.

The last time I saw him was off Le Havre in freak snow, the big flakes boiling around his head as he steered his ship into a storm which was roaring out of Germany as if the *Fimbulwinter* had already defeated the forces of life and we were witnessing the Twilight of the Gods. That was in 1932.

He told me he planned to leave his dhow in Hamburg for a while and then take the train east, via Berlin, with the thought that he would enjoy one last tour of his fatherland before coming home to die in Nuremberg. I assumed his words to be fanciful and that he spoke of retirement. He showed me a book. He said it contained a list of names. All those who were indebted to him, he said. All those who had betrayed his trust in them. Whole families, in some cases. I understood him to be some merchant's steward engaged to collect bad debts through the territories of the Holy Roman Empire.

I watched him go off under full sail. There was rime like diamonds on his rigging, the canvas gleamed like silver and snow was thick on his shoulders, a royal ermine. His fingers, sticking out of his tattered gloves like picked bones, seemed frozen to the wheel and his lank, grey hair stuck up in spikes, a halo.

I know now that I was the last Englishman to report an encounter with the Wandering Gentile, whose fame grew in those years, but I have since heard a little more of his story from others. The Gentile's expectations, it appears, were false. He still wanders the world, a ragged scarecrow, his eyes cold as iron, seeking the mysterious Isla de Juifes which, he swears, is protected by a supernatural glamour. The island he says can only be seen by his arch-rival's co-religionists. Moreover he blames climatic shifts for his further inconvenience. As you know, shortly after all this, the Haze vanished completely and our present tranquil age began . . .

Sexton Begg roused himself from his cousin's spell to interrupt. 'Not so tranquil if you're in corsair waters, to this day, old boy!'

Commander Begg agreed. 'If it were not for the corsairs ours would be a perfect world. But if it were to *remain* a perfect world we might find it necessary, perhaps, to introduce corsairs into it!'

'That sounds like a bit of a paradox,' declared Miss Sipp, a large woman with pre-Raphaelite hair.

Begg smiled. 'If we do not allow for paradoxes, my dears, we're doomed to repeat all our failures again and again. Just like the poor Gentile. Even with the prospect of fulfilment, he did not seem a happy man. And he has clearly learned nothing from his experiences. He repeats them over and over. Just like the poor old Gentile . . .'

'Has he never revisited the island?' Sir Sexton wished to know.

'Never,' said Begg. 'The Rose told me, the last time we met in Sporting Club Square, that nothing has ever changed. For some reason Count Manfred is blind to the island, even when he sails past it close enough to rip that old dhow's keel wide open. But the ship's protected by whatever keeps the poor devil alive and invulnerable, so it is never damaged. Yet the count is convinced his map is at fault. Or his informants. Or his crew. Whatever small sums he gets he always spends on larger or older or more detailed maps of those waters. And is always, of course, disappointed.'

'He never learned the lesson of Lazarus, then?' enquired Miss Sipp.

'Exactly,' agreed their narrator. 'It was not, I suppose, in his nature to rest.'

'And what of Las Cascadas – and Quelch?' Sir Sexton wished to know, waving his empty ballon as if to emphasise his curiosity.

'We live in a new and tranquil age,' said Commander Begg. 'The last time I returned to Las Cascadas the most urgent talking point was the outrageous price of fish. It's the same almost everywhere, these days.'

Then the old seadog paused, as if choosing his words carefully. 'Meanwhile, Captain Quelch and the Rose returned to their island stronghold. Which,' he concluded with a sigh of considerable relish, 'is quite a different story.'

EPILOGUE

On the Nature of Miracles

'. . . quite a different story,' repeated Commander Begg, smiling broadly, for he was once again at Las Cascadas, and Don Victor Dust's other guest was the Rose herself. These were in the days when the Haze was already being described as evidence of mass hysteria, 'and not for me to tell, my dear.'

Don Victor responded to this with his usual shy courtesy, 'Well, Countess, is it to remain your secret?'

'There's no secret, your excellency. After our encounter with Herr Lazarus and upon learning the nature of Count Manfred's singular doom, some of the magic left our romance and we were not to rediscover it until much later. But poor Horace never did get his other quarter-million ryads. What's more, you can imagine what the family thought of me when I had to admit that our ancestor was up and wandering again . . .'

'And the Lombardians?' asked Commander Begg.

'Something to do with the Pope. My father was a little vague about it. There was no great harm resulted, as far as I could tell.'

'A rather prosaic end to a marvellous tale,' said Don Victor. 'Or are we to hear of further miracles from the Wandering Jew?'

The Rose was amused. 'I asked him much the same question, your excellency, before we left the island. Indeed, I was very direct. I asked the Jew if he *could* work miracles. But he shook his head. "It seems to me," he said, "that legendary miracle-workers are always those who have been driven from the fold under some curse or other and are not generally recognised until after they are dead. Indeed, the fact of their banishment or execution adds to the authority of their legend!" In his experience it often becomes politically useful to revive a myth (if not a memory) and that dangerous psychopath of a generation gone becomes a lovable old uncle or a troubled boy with a heart of gold. The politically involved nun becomes a saint. The saint becomes a demon. And so on. He thought that most miracle-workers found their reputations enhanced by a distance in time and space. "People do love to dream, don't they?" he said. "I have no special powers, my dear – merely a little more experience than most. I was always of a placid disposition. They completely misjudged me, you know, from the very beginning of this. I wasn't *refusing* the poor boy a drink! Who could? I suspect he misheard me. I was merely asking him if he preferred lemonade or apple-juice?

'"And thus," concluded the Wandering Jew with a philosophical shrug, "thanks to a moment of middle-class insensitivity, I was damned to eternal life. Well, if that's God's idea of justice, I'm making the best of it. For all I know they're still arguing my case somewhere."'

'He seems eminently sane for one of such bizarre experience,' suggested Don Victor. 'Did the Jew offer you no special wisdom? No great secret drawn from all his millennia of existence?' Don Victor was a little sceptical of her reticence. 'Countess, did he tell you nothing else?'

'Only one thing,' said the Rose. 'It was perhaps the most startling narrative of them all. About a lustful abbess who, as penance, determined to discover if all trees were God or if there were evil trees as well. There were the familiar ingredients of innocence betrayed, loss, dispersal and festering revenge . . . The Jew called it the Tale of the Wandering Moslem and *her* story began, apparently, in the Sinai, a few centuries ago . . .'

But the tale the Rose told was meant only for her listeners and was never to be published.

That tale told, Sir Sexton Begg asked if they knew anything of the whereabouts of Mr Sam Oakenhurst, who had been Jack Karaquazian's best friend in that other, disintegrating world they had fled. It was Rose von Bek who answered, saying that he had left his luggage in her plane. When she had forced herself to sort through it, she had discovered a few damaged pages of crudely printed magazines. These were the V-mags with which for a long while Sam had been obsessed. What puzzled her, she said, was that Sam had no doubt read them and seen his own name there. Had he thought it a coincidence? Or had he read the story, as he often had, as some sort of oracle? Whatever the circumstances, the others agreed with her that there was something uncomfortable and chilling about fragments apparently written for a commercial medium and without any literary merit whatsoever. Some kind of parody of an old sf series, Edwin Begg thought. But Albert Begg was not sure he was right. Ultimately, the interpretation of the fragments had to do with the expectations and personality of the reader . . .

3. some fragments found in the effects of mr sam oakenhurst

Only the Lonely

'Bob's your uncle and Billy-Bob's your Revered Main type,' declared young Motherly Otherly that next morning, as the *Wonderful Steam* spiralled insouciantly through the scales on one of those calm, easy dives which never fails to relax even the most anxious Chaos Engineer.

'Slap me with a docket box,' roars big Sam Oakenhurst, on special download from his Mistress Original, the Merchant Venturer Pearl Peru who obtained him in peculiar circumstances. 'Is this thing primed?' He squints up the barrel of a rusting old Banning which sparks and burps into his face, clearly irritated but refusing to rise to Sam's goading. Sam has a fatal compulsion to tease grumpy old ordnance until it strikes out at him. It's what got him into trouble in the first place. He rubs abstractedly at his new radiation burns, pulsing cerise and lemon yellow on his darkening skin. A halo of fractal dust boils from his wriggling mouth and he frowns, trying to recall his role.

Professor Pop, smoothing his vast beard, frowns over the plans of his new Boomwapper. He grins in anticipation and sends for Little Rupoldo. His handsome favourite will both help him build and test the Boomwapper and take it, an effective counter-hubbub, into the shrill cacophony of the Drinking Bird, there to discover fresh colour. 'See Sam. We have ten billion new scales to explore. Our adventure can never end!'

This is unwelcome news to Sam, who longs for death as no

near-immortal ever longed before. But he has a role to perform. He flings himself down at his console and considers his ikons.

Correcting the Balance

'Let's have no more of this pointless rivalry.' Captain Quelch is magnanimous. After all, his elegant disintegrator-yacht swims at anchor in the nearest quadrant fold and he is making ready to escape a game being taken altogether too seriously for his taste. 'Surely it's better to find a happy compromise, than continue to fight a battle neither side can ever really win. We only appear to win. But we don't control the game any longer, do we, and that's what counts.' He creaks in his massive leathers which bear the stains of uncounted skirmishes and every major battle the multiverse has known. His jowls rasp against his shirt collar and he breathes with some difficulty, pulling on a hissing Anderson mask and buckling it with one hand as he reaches into his power trousers and harnesses the connectors.

Experimentally, Quelch flexes his monstrous wings which shine like green obsidian. '*Non nobis sed omnibus,* as they say, what?'

An odd expression comes into his bloodshot eyes and he flares his nostrils as if embarrassed by his own might.

Thoughtfully, Quelch murmurs, 'Goodbye, Mr Chips.' He is for a moment lost in his memories of simpler, more ordinary days.

CHAPTER FIVE MILLION NINE HUNDRED THOUSAND
AND FIFTY TWO (a)

At Odds With The Natural Order

Travellers through the Second Ether called Sahn-na-Horo 'The Port of Tears'. Her people were said to weep when they left her and to weep when they saw her again. Ethereal against the cold blue wastes of Tomkins' Bend, her impossibly slender minarets shimmered like a vast mirage, filling Uncle Bloodbelly's whole V and threatening to sink them under the weight of its unbearable magnificence. 'Ah! Aha!' sings Uncle B, his fangs bright and bleeding from overzealous cleaning. 'Oh! Oho! Korny, my dear. I'm not to be trapped with that old one. Come up with something better, dear. Something better, Korny, dear, please. I'm an old Chaos Engineer and my experience is often my enemy. What's the use of hanging on, I ask. Maybe I should let myself fall for your pathetic deception, Korny dear, and get it all over with. Ain't you bored as me, Korno?'

But Schultz was pecking at the screen with vapid, convulsive movements. 'Watch the farping equations come, Bloody Bloody Belly, and tell old Kaprikorn Schultz, respected banker to the Homeboy Tong, that he's lost his touch!' But Captain B was scarcely listening as he inspected the new meat. 'You complain to everyone about the quality and it does you no good at all. Equations, Korny?'

'Only the fundamental theorem you were all looking for, a couple of years or so ago, until you all got tired of it, or simply forgot what you had set off to do.'

'How do you mean?' asked Bloodbelly, at which the respected banker shrugged rather triumphantly: 'Forgot?'

He started as Little Rupoldo's excited features appeared on the V. 'Oh, pards! Oh, pards! Our virtue is rewarded. Quite by accident we have discovered a means of back-spiralling through the scales. We plan to share our discovery with all our comrades.'

Enter Pearl Peru, and Sam Oakenhurst is once again gratefully absorbed. Go to Code P . . .

'It's all I ever found,' the Rose told them, when they met the next day in Squire Begg's legendary Coffee Hall, fashioned out of one of the old artisans' workshops. 'Sam wanted death more than he wanted me.'

Privately, Colinda Dovero believed this to be an overstatement, but she allowed her friend a little melodrama, especially if she really did miss Sam Oakenhurst.

'Is there such a place as the Second Ether?' asked Aunt Poppy Begg suddenly. 'Or is it something we have all imagined?'

'Of course it's real, dear. Everything's real in the multiverse, you know.' Miss Sipp was amused at her old mistress's naïveté. 'You should be as aware of that as anyone, from what you've said to me over the years, dear.'

Poppy Begg smiled fondly at her memories.

'That reminds me of a story you might not yet have heard,' said Rose von Bek. 'A version of it was actually written as fiction by Warwick Begg, when he still lived over there in Crowley Mansions. It was one of the very few stories he wrote for *The Passing Show* magazine, but it was mysteriously "killed" by powers greater than the editor, apparently the chairman of Amalgamated Press, the publisher, and only recently came to light . . .'

4. *the black blade's summoning*

Come, Mephistophilis, let us dispute again,
And argue of divine Astrology.
Tell me, are there many Heavens above the moon?
Are all celestial bodies but one globe,
As is the substance of this centric earth?

Christopher Marlowe,
The Tragical History of Doctor Faustus

CHAPTER ONE

An Unusual Occurrence on the Xanardwys Road

The rider was lean, almost etiolated, but subtly muscled. His ascetic features were sensitive, his skin milk-white. From deep cavities within that half-starved face moody crimson eyes burned like the flowers of Hell. Once or twice he turned in his saddle to look back.

A tribe of Alofian hermaphrodites at his heels, the man rode eastward across the Dakwinsi Steppe, hoping to reach fabled Xanardwys before the snows blocked the pass.

His pale silver mare, hardiest of all Bastans, was bred to this terrain and had as determined a hold on life as the sickly albino who had to sustain himself by drugs or the stolen life-stuff of his fellows.

Drawing the black sealskin snow-cloak about him, the man set his face against the weather. His name was Elric and he was a prince in his own country, the last of his long line and without legitimate issue, an outcast almost everywhere in a world coming to hate and resent his alien kind as the power of Melniboné faded and the strength of the Young Kingdoms grew. He did not much care for his own safety but he was determined to live, to return to his island kingdom and be re-united with his sweet cousin Cymoril, whom he would one day marry. It was this ambition alone which drove him on through the blizzard.

Clinging to his horse's mane as the sturdy beast pressed against the deepening drifts which threatened to bury the world, Elric's senses grew as numb as his flesh. The mare moved slowly across the ridges, keeping to the high ground, heading always away from the afternoon sun. At night Elric dug them both a snow-hole and wrapped them in his lined canvasses. He carried the equipment of the Kardik, whose hunting grounds these were.

Elric no longer dreamed. He was almost entirely without conscious thought. Yet still his horse moved steadily towards Xanardwys, where hot springs brought eternal summer and where scarlet roses bloomed against the snow.

Towards evening on the fifth day of his journey, Elric became aware of an extra edge of coldness in the air. Though the great crimson disc of the setting sun threw long shadows over the white landscape, its light did not penetrate far. It now appeared to Elric that a vast wall of ice loomed up ahead, like the sides of a gigantic, supernatural fortress. There was something insubstantial about it. Perhaps Elric had discovered one of those monumental mirages which, according to the Kardik, heralded the inevitable doom of any witness.

Elric had faced more than one inevitable doom and felt no terror for this one, but his curiosity aroused him from the semi-stupor into which he had fallen. As they approached the towering ice he saw himself and his horse in perfect reflection. He smiled a grim smile, shocked by his own gauntness. He looked twice his real age and felt a hundred times older. Encounters with the supernatural had a habit of draining the spirit, as others whom he had met could readily testify . . .

Steadily his reflection grew larger until without warning he was swallowed by it – suddenly united with his own image! Then he was riding through a quiet, green dale which, he sincerely hoped, was the Valley of Xanardwys. He looked over his shoulder and saw a blue cloud billowing down a hillside and disappearing. Perhaps the mirror effect had something to do with the freakish weather of this region?

He was profoundly relieved that Xanardwys – or at least its valley – was proving a somewhat substantial legend. He dismissed all questions concerning the phenomenon which had brought him here and pressed on in good spirits. All around were the signs of spring – the warm, scented air, the bright wild-flowers, the budding trees and shrubs, the lush grass – and he marvelled at a wonderful paradox of geography which, according to the tales he'd heard, had saved many fugitives and travellers. Soon he must come to the ivory spires and ebony roofs of the city herself where he would rest, buy provisions, shelter and then continue his journey to Elwher, which lay beyond all the maps of his world.

The valley was narrow with steeply rising sides, like a tunnel, roots and branches of dark green trees tangling overhead in the soft earth. Elric felt a welcome sense of security and he drew deep breaths, relishing the sweet fecundity all around. This luxury of nature after the punishing ice brought him fresh vitality and new hope. Even his mare had developed a livelier gait.

However, when after an hour or two the sides grew yet steeper and narrower, the albino prince began to puzzle. He had never encountered such a natural phenomenon and indeed was beginning to believe that this gorgeous wealth of spring might be, after all, supernatural in origin. But then, even as he considered turning back and taking heed of a prudence he usually ignored, the sides of the valley began to sink to gentler rolling hills, widening to reveal in the distance a misty outline which must surely be that of Xanardwys.

After pausing to drink at a sparkling stream, Elric and his mare continued on. Now they crossed a vast stretch of greensward flanked by distant mountains, punctuated by stands of trees, flowery meadows, ponds and rivers. Slowly they came closer to the domestic reassurance of Xanardwys's rural rooftops.

Elric drew in a deep, contented sigh.

A great roaring erupted suddenly in Elric's ears and he was blinded as a new sun rose rapidly into the western sky, shrieking and wailing like a soul escaped from hell, multi-coloured flames forming a pulsing aura. Then the sound became a single, deep, sonorous chord, slowly fading.

Elric's horse stood mesmerised, as if turned to ice. The albino dismounted, cursing and throwing up his arm to protect his eyes. The broad rays stretched for miles across the landscape, bursting from the pulsing globe and carrying with them huge shapes, dark and writhing, seeming to struggle and fight even as they fell. And now the air was filled with an utterly horrifying noise, like the beating of a million

[43]

pairs of monstrous wings. Trumpets bellowed, the brazen voices of an army, heralding an even more horrible sound – the despairing moan of a whole world's souls voicing their agony, the fading shouts and dying cries of warriors in the last, weary stages of a battle.

Peering into the troubled vivacity of that mighty light, Elric felt heavy, muscular, gigantic forms, stinking with a sweet, bestial, almost overpowering odour, landing with massive thuds, shaking the ground with such force that the entire terrain threatened to collapse. This rain of monsters did not cease. It was only the purest of luck which saved Elric from being crushed under one of the falling bodies. He had the impression of metal ringing and clashing, of voices screaming and calling, of wings beating, beating, beating, like the wings of moths against a window, in a kind of frantic hopelessness. And still the monsters continued to fall out of a sky whose light changed subtly now, growing deeper and more stable until the entire world was illuminated by a steady, scarlet glare against which flying, falling shapes moved in black silhouette – wings, helmets, armour, swords – twisted in the postures of defeat. Now the predominant smell reminded Elric of the Fall and the sweet odour of rot, of the summer's riches returning to their origins, and still mingled with this was the fetid stink of angry brutes.

As the light became gentler and the great disc began to fade, Elric grew aware of other colours and more details. The stink alone threatened to steal his senses – the snorting, acrid breath of titanic beasts, threatening sudden death and alarming every revitalised fibre of his being. Elric glimpsed brazen scales, huge silvery feathers, hideously beautiful insect eyes and mouths, wondrously distorted, half-crystalline bodies and faces, like Leviathan and all his kin, emerging after millions of years from beneath a sea which had encrusted them with myriad colours and asymmetrical forms, made them moving monuments in coral, with faceted eyes which stared up in blind anguish at a sky through which still plunged, wings flapping, fluttering, folded or too damaged to bear their weight, the godlike forms of their supernatural kind. Clashing rows of massive fangs and uttering sounds whose depth and force alone was sufficient to shake the whole valley, to topple Xanardwys's towers, crack her walls and send her townsfolk fleeing with black blood boiling from every orifice, the monsters continued to fall.

Only Elric, inured to the supernatural, his senses and his body tuned to alien orchestrations, did not suffer the fate of those poor, unlucky creatures.

For mile upon mile in all directions, through light now turning to a bloody pink flecked with brass and copper, the landscape was crowded with the fallen titans: some on their knees; some supporting themselves upon swords, spears or shields; some stumbling blindly before collapsing over the bodies of their comrades; some lying still and breathing slowly, resting with wary relief as their eyes scanned the heavens. And still the mighty angels fell.

Elric, with all his experience, all the years of mystic study, could not imagine the immensity of the battle from which they fled. He, whose own patron Chaos Duke had the power to destroy all mortal enemies, attempted to imagine the collective power of this myriad army, each common soldier of which might belong to Hell's aristocracy. For these were the very Lords of Chaos, each one of whom had a vast and complex constituency. Of that, Elric was certain.

He realised that his heart was beating rapidly and he was breathing in brief, painful gasps. Deliberately he took control of himself, convinced that the mere presence of that battered host must ultimately kill him. Determined, at least, to experience all he could before he was consumed by the casual power of the monsters, Elric was about to step forward when he heard a voice behind him. It was human, it was sardonic, and its accent was subtly queer, but it used the High Speech of Old Melniboné.

'I've seen a few miracles in my travels, sir, but by heavens, it must be the first time I've witnessed a shower of angels. Can you explain it, sir? Or are you as mystified as me?'

CHAPTER TWO

A Dilemma Discovered in Xanardwys

The stranger was roughly the same height and build as Elric, with delicate, tanned features and pale blue eyes, sharp as steel. He wore the loose, baggy, cream-coloured clothing of some outland barbarian, belted with brown leather and a pouch which doubtless holstered some weapon or charm. He wore a broad-brimmed hat the colour of his shirt and breeches and he carried over his right shoulder another strange-looking weapon, or perhaps a musical instrument, all walnut, brass and steel. 'Are you a denizen of these parts, sir, or have you been dragged, like me, through some damnable chaos vortex against your will? I am Count Renark von Bek, late of the Rim. And you, sir?'

'Prince Elric of Melniboné. I believed myself in Xanardwys, but now I doubt it. I am lost, sir. What do you make of this?'

'If I were to call upon the mythology and religion of my ancestors, I would say we looked at the defeated Host of Chaos, the very archangels who banded with Lucifer to challenge the power of God. All peoples tell their own stories of such a war amongst the angels, doubtless echoes of some true event. So they say, sir. Do you travel the moonbeams, as I do?'

'The question's meaningless to me.' Elric's attention was focused upon just one of the thousands of Chaos Lords. They lay everywhere now, darkening the hills and plains as far as the horizon. He had recognised certain aspects of the creature well enough to identify him as Arioch, his own patron Duke of Hell.

Count von Bek became curious. 'What do you see, Prince Elric?'

The albino paused, his mind troubled. There was a mystery to all this which he could not understand and which he was too terrified to want to understand. He yearned with all his being to be elsewhere, anywhere but here; yet his feet were already moving, taking him through the groaning ranks whose huge bodies towered above him, seeking out his patron. 'Lord Arioch? Lord Arioch?'

A frail distant voice. 'Ah, sweetest of my slaves. I thought thee dead. Has thou brought me sustenance, darling heart? Sweetmeats for thy lord?'

There was no mistaking Lord Arioch's tone, but the voice had never been weaker. Was Lord Arioch already considering his own paradoxical death?

'I have no blood, no souls for thee today, great Duke.' Elric made his way towards a massive figure lying panting across a hillside. 'I am as weak as thee.'

'Then I love thee not. Begone . . .' The voice became nothing but fading echoes, even as Elric approached its source. 'Go back, Elric. Go back whence ye came . . . It is not thy time . . . Thou shouldst not be here . . . Beware . . . Obey me or I shall . . .' But the threat was empty and both knew it. Arioch had used all his strength.

'I would gladly obey thee, Duke Arioch.' Elric spoke feelingly. 'For I have a notion that even an adept in sorcery could not survive long in a world where so much Chaos dwells. But I know not how. I came here by an accident. I thought myself in Xanardwys.'

There was a pause, then a painful gasp of words. 'This . . . is . . . Xanardwys . . . but not that of thy realm. There is no . . . hope . . .

[46]

here. Go . . . go . . . back. There . . . is . . . no hope . . . This is the very end of Time . . . It is cold . . . so . . . cold . . . Thy destiny . . . does . . . not . . . lie . . . here . . .'

'Lord Arioch?' Elric's voice was urgent. 'I told thee . . . I know not how to return.'

The massive head lowered, regarding him with the complex eyes of the fly, but no sound came from his sweet, red lips of youth. Duke Arioch's skin was like shifting mercury, roiling upon his body, giving off sparks and auras and sudden bursts of brilliant, multi-coloured dust, reflecting the invisible fires of hell. And Elric knew that if his patron had manifested himself in all his original ·glory, not in this sickly form, Elric's very soul would have been consumed by the demon's presence. Duke Arioch was even now gathering his strength to speak again. 'Thy sword . . . has . . . the . . . power . . . to carve a gateway . . . to . . . the road home . . .' The vast mouth opened to drag in whatever atmosphere sustained its monstrous body. Silver teeth rattled like a hundred thousand arrows; the red mouth erupted with heat and stink, sufficient to drive the albino back. Oddly coloured wisps of flame poured from the nostrils. The voice was full of weary irony. 'Thou art . . . too . . . valuable to me, sweet Elric . . . Now I need all my allies . . . even mortals. This battle . . . must be . . . our last . . . against . . . against the power . . . of . . . the . . . Balance . . . and those who have . . . allied themselves . . . with it . . . those vile servants of Singularity . . . who would reduce all the substance of . . . the multiverse . . . to one, dull, coherent agony of boredom . . .'

This speech took the last of his energy. One final gasp, a painful gesture. 'Sing the song . . . the sword's song . . . sing together . . . that power will break thee into . . . the roads . . .'

'Lord Arioch, I cannot understand thee. I must know more.'

But the huge eyes had grown dull and it seemed some kind of lid had folded over them. Lord Arioch slept, or faded into death. And Elric wondered at the power that could bring low one of the great Chaos Lords. What power could extinguish the life-stuff of invulnerable immortals? Was that the power of the Balance? Or merely the power of Law – which the Lords of Entropy called 'The Singularity'? Elric had only a glimmering of the motives and ambitions of those mighty forces.

He turned to find von Bek standing beside him. The man's face was grim and he held his strange instrument in his two hands, as if to defend himself. 'What did the brute tell you, Prince Elric?'

Elric had spoken a form of High Melnibonéan, developed through the millennia as a means of intercourse between mortal and demon.

'Little that was concrete. I believe we should head for what remains of the city. These weary lords of hell seem to have no interest in it.'

Count Renark agreed. The landscape still resounded with the titanic clank of sword against shield and the thunderous descent of an armoured body, the smack of great wings and the stink of their breath. The stink was unavoidable, for what they expelled – dust, vapours, showers of fluttering flames and noxious gases of all descriptions – shrouded the whole world. Like mice running amongst the feet of elephants, the two men stumbled through shadows, avoiding the slow, weary movements of the defeated host. All around them the effects of Chaos grew manifest. Ordinary rocks and trees were warping and changing. Overhead the sky was a raging cacophony of lightnings, bellowings, and agitated, brilliantly coloured clouds. Yet somehow they reached the fallen walls of Xanardwys. Here corpses were already transforming, taking on something of the shapes of those who had brought this catastrophe with them when they fell through the multiverse, tearing the very fabric of reality as they descended, ruined and defeated.

Elric knew that soon these corpses would become re-animated with the random Chaos energy which, while insufficient to help the Chaos Lords themselves, was more than enough to give a semblance of life to a thing which had been mortal.

Even as von Bek and Elric watched, they saw the body of a young woman liquefy and then reform itself so that it still had something human about it but was now predominantly a mixture of bird and ape.

'Everywhere Chaos comes,' said Elric to his companion. 'It is always the same. These people died in agony and now they are not even allowed the dignity of death . . .'

'You're a sentimentalist, sir,' Count Renark spoke a little ironically.

'I have no feeling for these folk,' Elric assured him with rather too much haste. 'I merely mourn the waste of it all.' Stepping over metamorphosing bodies and fallen architecture, which also began to alter its shape, the two men reached a small, domed structure of marble and copper, seemingly untouched by the rest of Chaos.

'Some kind of temple, no doubt,' said von Bek.

'And almost certainly defended by sorcery,' added the albino, 'for no other building remains in one piece. We had best approach with a little caution.'

And he placed a hand up on his runesword, which stirred and murmured and seemed to moan for blood. Von Bek glanced towards the sword and a small shudder passed through his body. Then he led the way towards the temple. Elric wondered if this were some kind of entrance back to his own world. Had that been what Arioch meant? 'These are singularly unpleasant manifestations of Chaos,' Count von Bek was saying. 'This, surely, is Chaos gone sour – all that was virtue turned to vice. I have seen it more than once – in individuals as in civilisations.'

'You have travelled much, Count von Bek?'

'It was for many years my profession to wander, as it were, between worlds. I play the Game of Time, sir. As, I presume, do you.'

'I play no games, sir. Does your experience tell you if this building marks a route away from this realm and back to my own?'

'I could not quite say, sir. Not knowing your realm, for instance.'

'Sorcery protects this place,' said the albino, reaching for the hilt of his runesword. But Stormbringer uttered a small warning sound, as if to tell him that it could not be employed against this odd magic. Count von Bek had stepped closer and was inspecting the walls.

'See here, Prince Elric. There is a science at work. Look. Something alien to Chaos, perhaps?' He indicated seams in the surface of the building and, taking out a small folding knife, he scratched at it, revealing metal. 'This place has always had a supernatural purpose.'

As if the traveller had triggered some mechanism, the dome above them began to spin, a pale blue aura spreading from it and encompassing them before they could retreat. They stood unmoving as a door in the base opened and a human figure regarded them. It was a creature almost as bizarre as any Elric had seen before, with the same style of clothing as von Bek, but with a peaked, grubby white cap on its unruly hair, stubble upon its chin, its eyes bloodshot but sardonically intelligent, a piece of charred root (doubtless some tribal talisman) still smouldering in the corner of his mouth. 'Greetings, dear sirs. You seem as much in a pickle over this business as I am. Don't it remind you a bit of Milton, what? "Cherub and Seraph rolling in the flood, with scattered arms and ensigns?" Paradise lost, indeed, my dear comrades in adversity. And I would guess that is not all we are about to lose . . . Will you step inside?'

The eccentric stranger introduced himself as Captain Quelch, a soldier of fortune, who had been in the middle of a successful arms sale when he had found himself falling through space, to arrive within the building. 'I have a feeling it's this old fellow's fault, gentlemen.'

The interior was simple. It was bathed in a blue light from above and contained no furniture or evidence of ritual. There was a plain geometric design on the floor and coloured windows set high near the roof.

The place was filled with children of all ages, gathered around an old man who lay near the centre of the temple, on the tiles.

He was clearly dying. He beckoned for Elric to approach. It was as if he, like the lords of Chaos, had been drained of all his life-stuff. Elric knelt down and asked if there were anything he needed, but the old man shook his head. 'Only a promise, sir. I am Patrius, High Priest of Donblas the Justice Maker. I was able to save these, of all Xanardwys's population, because they were attending my class. I drew on the properties of this temple to throw a protection around us. But the effort of making such desperate and powerful magic has killed me, I fear. All I wish now is that you take the children to safety. Find a way out of this world, for soon it must collapse into unformed matter, into the primal stuff of Chaos. It is inevitable. There is no hope for this realm, sir. Chaos devours us.'

A dark-skinned girl began to weep at this and the old man reached out his hand to comfort her.

'She weeps for her parents,' said the old man. 'She weeps for what became of them and what they will become. All these children have second sight. I have tutored them in the ways of the multiverse. Take them to the roads, sir. They will survive, I am sure. It is all you need do. Lead them to the roads!'

A silence fell. The old man died.

Elric murmured to von Bek – 'Roads? He entrusts me with a task that's meaningless to me.'

'Not to me, Prince Elric.' Von Bek was looking warily in Captain Quelch's direction. The man had climbed a stone stair and stood peering out of the windows in the direction of the defeated legions of hell. He seemed to be talking to himself in a foreign language.

'You understood the elder? You know a way out of this doomed place?'

'Aye, Prince Elric. I told you. I am an adept. A jugador. I play the Game of Time and roam the roads between the worlds. I sense that you are a comrade – perhaps even more than that – and that you are unconscious of your destiny. It is not my place to reveal anything to you more than is necessary – but if you would join with me in the Game of Time, become a mukhamir, then you have only to say.'

'My interest is in returning to my own sphere and to the woman I love,' said Elric simply. He reached out a long-fingered, bone-white hand, on which throbbed a single Actorios, and touched the hair of the sobbing child. It was a gesture which gave the watching von Bek much insight into the character of this moody lord. The girl looked up, her eyes desperate for reasssurance, but she found little hope in the ruby orbs of the alien creature who stared down at her, his expression full of loss, of yearning for some impossible ambition. Yet she spoke: 'Will you save us, sir?'

'Madam,' said the Prince of Ruins, with a small smile and a bow, 'I regret that I am in a poor position to save myself, let alone an entire college of tyro seers, but it is in my self-interest that we should all be free of this. That you can be sure of . . .'

Captain Quelch came down the steps with an awkward swagger and a hearty, if unconvincing, chuckle. 'We'll be out of this in no time, little lady, be certain of that.'

But it was Elric to whom the young woman still looked and it was to Elric she spoke. 'I am called Far-Seeing and First-of-Her-Kind. The former name explains my skills. The latter explains my future and is mysterious to me. You have the means of saving us, sir. That I can see.'

'A young witch!' Captain Quelch chuckled again, this time with an odd note, almost of self-reference. 'Well, my dear. We are certainly saved, with so much sorcery at our disposal!'

Elric met the eyes of Far-Seeing and was almost shocked by the beauty he saw there. She was, he knew, part of his destiny. But perhaps not yet. Perhaps not ever, if he failed to escape the doom which came relentlessly to Xanardwys. They were in no immediate danger from the Chaos Lords; only from the demons' unconscious influence, which gave foul vitality to the very folk they had killed, transforming them into travesties. Casually, unknowingly, the aristocracy of hell was destroying its own sanctuary, as mortals, equally unknowingly, poison their own wells with their waste. Such brute behaviour horrified Elric and made him despair. Perhaps after all, we were mere toys in the hands of mad, immortal beasts? Beasts without conscience or motive.

This was no time for abstract introspection! Even as he looked behind him, Elric saw the walls of the temple begin to shudder, lose substance, and then reform. But those within had nowhere to flee. They heard grunts and howls from outside.

Shambling Chaos creatures pawed at the building, their sensibilities too crude to be challenged by argument, science or sorcery. The revived citizens of Xanardwys now only knew blind need, a horrible hunger to devour any form of flesh. By that means alone could they keep even this faint grip on life and what they had once been. They were driven by the knowledge of utter and everlasting extermination; their souls unjustly damned, mere fodder for the Lords of Hell.

Once, Elric's folk had made a pact with Chaos in all her vital glory, in all her power and magnificent creativity. They had seen only the golden promise of Chaos, not the vile decadence which greed and blind ambition could make of it. Yet, when they had discovered Evil and married that to Chaos, then the true immorality of their actions had become plain to all save themselves. They had lost the will to see beyond their own culture and convictions, their own needs and brute survival. Their decadence was all too evident to the Young Kingdoms and to one sickly inheritor of the Ruby Throne, Elric; who, yearning to know how his great people had turned to cruel and melancholy incest, had left his inheritance in the keeping of his cousin; had left the woman he loved beyond life to seek an answer to his questions . . . But, he reflected, instead he had come to Xanardwys to die.

Renark von Bek was running for the steps, his weapon in his hands. Even as he reached the top a creature, flapping on leathery wings in parody of the Chaos Lords, burst through the window. Von Bek threw his weapon to his shoulder. There was a sharp report and the creature screamed, falling backwards with a great, ragged wound in its head. 'Angel shot,' called von Bek. 'I carry nothing else, these days.' Quelch seemed to understand him and approve.

While he could not grasp the nature of the weapon, Elric was grateful for it, for now the door of the temple bulged inward.

He felt a soft hand on his wrist. He looked down to see the girl staring up at him. 'Your sword must sing its song,' she said. 'This I know. Your sword must sing its song – and you must sing with it. You must sing together. It will give us our road.' Her eyes were unfocused. She saw into the future, as Arioch had done, or was it the past? She spoke distantly. Elric knew he was in the presence of a great natural psychic – but still her words hardly made sense to him.

'Aye – the sword will be singing, my lady, soon enough,' he said as he caressed her hair, longing for his youth, his happiness and his Cymoril. 'But I fear you'll not favour the tune Stormbringer plays.' Gently he pushed her to go with the children and comfort them. Then his right arm swung like a heavy pendulum and his right gauntlet settled upon the black hilt of his runesword until, with a single, sudden movement, he drew the blade from its scabbard and Stormbringer gave a yelp of glee, like a thirsty hound craving blood.

'These souls are mine, Lord Arioch!'

But he knew that, ironically, he would be stealing a little of his patron's own life-stuff; for that was what animated these Chaos creatures, their bizarre deformities creating an obscene forest of flesh as they pressed through the doorway of the temple. That energy which had already destroyed this realm also gave a semblance of life to the creeping half-things which now confronted Elric and von Bek. Captain Quelch, claiming that he had no weapon, had gone to stand with the children, his arms out in a parody of protection. 'Good luck with that elephant gun, old man,' he said to Count von Bek, who lifted the weapon to his shoulder, took careful aim, squeezed the trigger and, in his own words, 'put a couple of pounds of Purdy's best into the blighters.' There was a hideous splash of ichor and soft flesh. Elric stepped away fastidiously as his companion again took aim and again pounded the horrible creatures back from the door. 'Though I think it fair to warn you, Prince Elric, that I only have a couple more of these left. After that, it's down to the old Smith and Wesson, I'm afraid.' And he tapped the pouch at his belt.

But the weapon was needed elsewhere as, against all the windows high in the walls, there came a rattling of scales and a scratching of claws and von Bek fell back to cover the centre while Elric stepped forward, his black runesword moaning with anticipation, pulsing with dark fire, its runes writhing and skipping in the unholy metal, the whole terrible weapon independent within the grip of its wielder, possessed of a profound and sinister life of its own, rising and falling now as the white prince moved against the Chaos creatures, drinking their life-stuff. What remained of their souls passed directly into the deficient body of the Melnibonéan, whose own eyes blazed in that unwholesome glory, whose own lips were drawn back in a wolfish snarl, his body splashed from head to foot with the filthy fluids of his post-human antagonists.

The sword began to utter a great, triumphant dirge as its thirst was satisfied, and Elric howled too, the ancient battle shouts of his people, calling upon the aristocracy of hell, upon its patron demons, and upon Lord Arioch, as the malformed corpses piled themselves higher and higher in the doorway, while von Bek's weapons banged and cracked, defending the windows.

'These things will keep attacking us,' called von Bek. 'There's no end to them. We must escape. It is our only hope, else we shall be overwhelmed soon enough.'

Elric agreed. He leaned, panting, on his blade, regarding his hideous work, his eyes cold with a death-light, his face a martial mask. 'I have a distaste for this kind of butchery,' he said. 'But I know nothing else to do.'

'You must take the sword to the centre,' said a pure, liquid voice. It was the girl, Far-Seeing.

She left the group, pushing past an uncertain Captain Quelch and reaching fearlessly out to the pulsing sword, its alien metal streaming with corrupted blood. 'To the centre.'

Von Bek, Captain Quelch and the other children stared in amazed silence as the girl's hand settled upon that awful blade, drawing it and its wielder through their parting ranks to where the corpse of the old man lay.

'The centre lies beneath his heart,' said Far-Seeing. 'You must pierce his heart and drive the sword beyond his heart. Then the sword will sing and you will sing, too.'

'I know nothing of any sword song,' said Elric again, but his protest was a ritual one. He found himself trusting the tranquil certainty of the girl, her deft movements, the way she guided him until he stood straddling the peaceful body of the master wizard.

'He is rich with the best of Law,' said Far-Seeing. 'And it is that stuff which, for a while, will fill your sword and make it work for us, perhaps even against its own interests.'

'You know much of my sword, my lady,' said Elric, puzzled.

The girl closed her eyes. 'I am against the sword and I am of the sword and my name is Swift Thorn.' Her voice was a chant, as if another occupied her body. She had no notion of the meaning of the words which issued from her. 'I am for the sword and I replace the sword. I am of the sisters. I am of the Just. It is our destiny to turn the ebony to silver, to seek the light, to create justice.'

Von Bek leaned forward. Far-Seeing's words seemed to have important meaning to him and yet he was clearly astonished at hearing them at all. He passed his hand before her eyes.

All attention was on her. Even Quelch's face had grown serious, while outside came the sounds of the Chaos creatures preparing for a fresh attack.

Then she was transformed, her face glowing with a pink-gold radiance, bars of silver light streaming from hair that seemed on fire, her rich, dark skin vibrant with supernatural life. 'Strike!' she cried. 'Strike, Prince Elric. Strike to the heart, to the centre! Strike now or our future is forever forbidden us!'

There came a guttural cough from the doorway. They had an impression of a jewelled eye, a wriggling red mouth, and they knew that some rogue Chaos Lord, scenting blood and souls, had determined to taste them for himself.

CHAPTER THREE

Walking Between the Worlds

'Strike! O, my lord! Strike!'

The girl's voice rang out, a pure, golden chord against the cacophony of Chaos, and she guided the black sword's fleshly iron towards the old man's heart.

'Strike, my lord. And sing your song!'

Then she made a movement with her palms and the runesword plunged downwards, plunged into the heart, plunged through sinew and bone and flesh into the very stone beneath and suddenly, through that white alchemy, a pale blue flame began to burn within the blade, gradually turning to pewter and fiery bronze, then to a brilliant, steady, silver.

Von Bek gasped. 'The sword of the archangel himself!'

But Elric had no time to ask what he meant for now the transformed runesword burned brighter still, blinding the children who whimpered and fell back before it, making Captain Quelch curse and grumble that he was endangered, while the girl was suddenly gone, leaving only her voice behind, lifted in a song of extraordinary beauty and spiritual purity; a song which seemed to ring from the steel itself; a song so wonderful, speaking of such joys and fulfilment, that Elric felt his heart lifting, even as the Chaos Lord's long, grey tongue flicked at his heels. From somewhere within him all the longing he had known, all the sadness and the grief and the loneliness, all his aspirations and dreams, his times of intense happiness, his loves and his hatreds, his affections and his dislikes, all were voiced in the same music which issued from his throat, as if his whole being had been concentrated into this single song. It was a victory and a plea. It was a celebration and an agony. It was nothing more nor less than the Song of Elric, the song of a single, lonely individual in an uncertain world, the song of a troubled intellect and a generous heart, of the last lord of his people, the brooding prince of ruins, the White Wolf of Melniboné.

And most of all, it was a song of love, of yearning idealism and desperate sadness for the fate of the world.

The silver light blazed brighter still and at its centre, where the old man's body had been and where the blade still stood, there now hovered a chalice of finely wrought gold and silver, its rim and base

[55]

emblazoned with precious stones which themselves emitted powerful rays. Elric, barely able to cling to the sword as the white energy poured through him, heard Count von Bek cry out in recognition. And then the vision was gone. And blackness, fine and silky as a butcher's familiar, spread away in all directions, as if they stood at the very beginning of Time, before the coming of the Light.

Then, as they watched, it seemed that spiders spun gleaming web after web upon that black void, filling it with their argent silk.

They saw shapes emerging, connected by the webs, filling the vacuum, crowding it, enriching it with wonder and colour, countless mighty spheres and curving roads and an infinite wealth of experience.

'This,' said Renark von Bek, 'is what we can make of Chaos. Here is the multiverse; those webs you see are the wide roads that pass between the realms. We call them "moonbeams" and it is here that creatures trade from world to world and where ships arrive from the Second Ether, bringing cargoes of terrible, exquisite stuffs not meant for mortal eyes. Here are the infinite realms, all the possibilities, all the best and the worst that can be in God's creation . . .'

'You do your deity credit, sir,' said Elric.

Von Bek made a graceful movement of his hand, like an elegant showman.

Forms of every kind blossomed before him, stretching to infinity – nameless colours, flaming and shimmering and glowing, or dull and distant and cold – complex spiderwebs stretching through all dimensions, one connected with another, glinting, quivering and delicate, yet bearing the cargo and traffic of countless millions of realms.

'There are your moonbeams, sir.' Von Bek was grinning like an ape and relishing this vast, varied, yet ultimately ordered multiverse, forever fecund, forever reproducing, forever expanding its materials derived from the raw, unreasoning, unpredictable stuff of Chaos, which mighty alchemy made concrete. This was the ultimate actuality, the fundamental reality on which all other realities were based, which most mortals only glimpsed in visions, in dreams, in an echo from deep within. 'The webs between the worlds are the great roads we tread to pass from one realm of the multiverse to another.'

Spheres blossomed and erupted, reformed and blossomed again. Swirling, half-familiar images reproduced themselves over and over in every possible variety and on every scale. Elric saw worlds in the shape of trees, galaxies like flowers, star systems which had grown together, root and branch, so tangled that they had become one huge, irregular planet; universes which were steely oceans; universes of unstable fire; universes of desolation and cold evil; universes of pulsing colour whose beings passed through flames to take benign and holy shapes; universes of gods and angels and devils; universes of vital tranquillity; universes of shame, of outrage, of humiliation and contemplative courtesy; universes of perpetually raging Chaos, of exhausted, sterile Law; all dominated by a sentience which they themselves had spawned. The multiverse had become entirely dependent for its existence on the reasoning powers, the desires and terrors, the courage and moral resolve of its inhabitants. One could no longer exist without the other.

And still a presence could be sensed behind all this: the presence which held in its hand the scales of justice, the Cosmic Balance, forever tilting this way or that, towards Law or towards Chaos, and always stabilised by the struggles of mortal beings and their super-natural counterparts, their unseen, unknown sisters and brothers in all the mysterious realms of the multiverse.

'Have you heard of a Guild of Adepts calling itself "the Just"?' asked von Bek, still as stone and drinking in this familiar vision, this infinite constituency, as another might kneel upon his native earth. Since his companions did not reply, he continued, 'Well, my friends, I am of that persuasion. I trained in Alexandria and Marrakech. I have learned to walk between the realms. I have learned to play the *Zeitjuego*, the Game of Time. Grateful as I am for your wizardry, sir, you should know that your skills drew unconsciously upon all this. You are able to perform certain rituals, describe certain openings through which you summon aid from other realms. You define these allies in terms of unsophisticated, even primitive superstition. You, sir, with all your learning and experience, do little else. But if you come with me and play the great Game of Time, I will show you all the wonders of this multiverse. I will teach you how to explore it and manipulate it and remember it – for without training, without the long years in which one learns the craft of the mukhamir, the mortal mind cannot grasp and contain all it witnesses.'

'I have things to do in my own realm,' Elric told him. 'I have responsibilities and duties.'

'I respect your decision, sir,' said von Bek with a bow, 'though I regret it. You would have made a noble player in the Game. Yet, however unconsciously, I think you have always played and will continue to play.'

'Well, sir,' said Elric, 'I believe you intend to honour me and I thank you. Now I would appreciate it if you would put me on the right road to my realm.'

'I'll take you back there myself, sir. It's the least I can do.'

Elric would not, as von Bek had predicted, remember the details of his journey between the realms. It would come to seem little more than a vague dream, yet now he had the impression of constant proliferation, of the natural and supernatural worlds blending and becoming a single whole. Monstrous beings prowled empty spaces of their own making. Whole nations and races and worlds experienced their histories in the time it took Elric to put one foot in front of another upon the silver moonbeams, that delicate, complicated lacework of roads. Shapes grew and decayed, translated and trans-mogrified, becoming at once profoundly familiar and disturbingly strange. He was aware of passing other travellers upon the silver roads; he was aware of complex societies and unlikely creatures, of communicating with some of them. Walking with a steady, deter-mined gait, von Bek led the albino onward. 'Time is not measured as you measure it,' the guide senser explained. 'Indeed, it is scarcely measured at all. One rarely requires it as one walks between the worlds.'

'But what is this – this multiverse?' Elric shook his head. 'It's too much for me, sir. I doubt my brain is trained enough to accept it at all!'

'I can help you. I can take you to the *medersim* of Alexandria or of Cairo, of Marrakech and Malador, there to learn the skills of the adept, to learn all the moves in the great Game of Time.'

Again the albino shook his head.

With a shrug von Bek returned his attention to the children. 'But what are we to do with these?'

'They'll be safe enough with me, old boy.' Captain Quelch spoke from behind them. The floor of the temple alone remained, hovering in space, with the children gathered upon it. At their centre now stood Far-Seeing, smiling, her arms extended in a gesture of protection. 'We'll find a safe little harbour, my dears.'

'Have you power over all this, Count Renark?' Elric asked.

'It is within the power of all mortals to manipulate the multiverse, to create reality, to make justice and order out of the raw stuff of Chaos. Yet without Chaos there would be no Creation, and perhaps no Creator. That is the simple truth of all existence, Lord Elric. The promise of immortality. It is possible to affect one's own destiny. That is the hope Chaos offers us.' Von Bek kept a wary eye upon Quelch, who seemed aggrieved.

'If you'll forgive me interrupting this philosophical discourse, old sport, I must admit to being concerned for my own safety and future and that of the little children for whom I now have responsibility.

You gentlemen have affairs of multiversal magnitude to concern you, but I am the only guardian of these orphans. What are we to do? Where are we to go?' There were tears in Quelch's eyes. His own plight had moved him to some deep emotion.

The girl called Far-Seeing laughed outright at Captain Quelch's protestations. 'We need no such guardianship as yours, my lord.'

Captain Quelch made a crooked grin and reached towards her.

Whereupon the temple floor vanished and they all stood upon a broad, bright road, stretching through the multi-coloured multitude of spheres and planes, that great spectrum of unguessable dimensions, staring at Quelch.

'I'll take the children, sir,' said Count von Bek. 'I have an idea I know where they will be safe and where they can improve their skills without interference.'

'What are you suggesting, sir?' Captain Quelch bridled as if accused. 'Do you find me insufficiently responsible . . .?'

'Your motives are suspect, my lord.' Again Far-Seeing spoke, her pure tones seeming to fill the whole multiverse. 'I suspect you want us only that you may eat us.'

Elric, baffled by the girl's words, glanced at von Bek, who shrugged in helpless uncertainty. There was a confrontation taking place between the child and the man.

'To eat you, my dear? Ha, ha! I'm old Captain Quelch, not some cannibal troll.'

The white road blazed on every side.

Elric felt frail and vulnerable beneath the gaze of that multiplicity of spheres and realms. He could barely keep his sanity in the face of so many sudden changes, so much new knowledge. He thought that Captain Quelch's features twisted, faded a little and then became quite a different shape, with eyes that reminded him of Arioch's. Then, just as von Bek realised the same thing, Elric knew they had been duped. This creature could still change its shape!

A Chaos Lord, no doubt, who had not been as badly wounded as the others, who had scented the life-stuff within the temple and found a way of admittance. Perhaps it was Quelch who had drained the old man of life and had failed to feed on the children only because the girl unconsciously resisted him. The children gathered around her, forming a compact circle. Their eyes glared into those of an insect, into the very face of the Fly. Now Quelch's body shifted and trembled and quaked and cracked and took its true, bizarrely baroque shape, all asymmetrical carapace and coruscating scales, brass feathery wings, the same obscene stink which had filled the Xanardwys Valley; as if he could keep his human shape no longer, must burst back into his true form, hungering for souls, craving every scrap of mortal essence to feed his depleted veins.

'If you seek to escape your Conqueror's vengeance, my lord, you are mistaken,' said the girl. 'You are already condemned. See what you have become. See what you would feed off to sustain your life. Look upon what you would destroy – upon what you once wished to be. Look upon all this and remember, Lord Demon, that this is what you have turned your back upon. It is not yours. We are not yours. You cannot feed off us. Here we are free and powerful as you. But you never deceived me, for I am called Far-Seeing and First-of-Her-Kind and now I sense my destiny, which is to live my own tale. For it is by our stories that we create the reality of the multiverse and by our faith that we sustain it. Your tale is almost ended, great Lord of Chaos—'

And at this she was surprised by the great beast's bawling mockery, its only remaining weapon against her. It shook with mephitic mirth, its scales clattering and switching. It clutched at a minor triumph.

'It is you who are mistaken, my Lady Far-Seeing. I am not of Chaos! I am Chaos's enemy. I fought well but was caught up with them as they fell. Their master is not my master. I serve the great Singularity, the Harbinger of Final Order, the Original Insect. I am Quelch and I am, foolish girl, *a Lord of Law*! It is my party which would *abolish* Chaos. We fight for complete control of the Cosmic Balance. Nothing less. Those Chaos Engineers, those adventurers, those rebellious rogues and corsairs who have so plagued the Second Ether, I am their nemesis!' The monstrous head turned, almost craftily. 'Can you not see how different I am?'

In truth, Elric and von Bek could see only similarity. This Quelch of Law was identical in appearance to Arioch of Chaos. Even their hatreds and ambitions seemed alike.

'It is sometimes impossible to understand the differences between' the parties,' murmured von Bek to Elric. 'They have fought so long they have become almost the same thing. This, I think, is decadence. It is time, I suspect, for the Conjunction.' He explained nothing and Elric desired to know no more.

Lord Quelch now towered above them, constantly licking lips glittering with fiery saliva, scratching at his crystalline carapace, his moody, insect eyes searching the reaches of the multiverse, perhaps for allies.

'I can call upon the Authority of the Great Singularity,' Lord Quelch boasted. 'You are powerless. I must feed. I must continue my work. Now I will eat you.'

One reptilian foot stepped forward, then another as he bore down upon the gathered children, while Far-Seeing stared back bravely in an attitude of challenge. Then von Bek and Elric had moved between the monster and its intended prey. Stormbringer still shone with the remaining grey-green light of its white sorcery, still murmured and whispered in Elric's grasp.

Lord Quelch turned his attention upon the albino prince. 'You took what was mine. I am a Lord of Law. The old man had what I must have. I must survive. I must continue to exist. The fate of the multiverse depends upon it. What is that to the sacrifice of a few young occultists? Law believes in the power of reason, the measurement and control of all natural forces, the husbandry of our resources. I must continue the fight against Chaos. Once millions gave themselves up in ecstasy to my cause.'

'Once, perhaps, your cause was worthy of their sacrifice,' said von Bek quietly. 'But too much blood has been spilt in this terrible war. Those of you who refuse to speak of reconciliation are little more than brutes and deserve nothing of the rest of us, save our pity and our contempt.'

Elric wondered at this exchange. Even when reading the most obscure of his people's grimoires, he could never have imagined witnessing such a confrontation between a mortal and a demigod.

Lord Quelch snarled again. Again he turned his hungry insect's eyes upon his intended prey. 'Just one or two, perhaps?'

Neither Elric nor von Bek were required to defend the children. Quelch was cowering before the gaze of Far-Seeing, increasingly frightened, as if he only now understood the power he was confronting. 'I am hungry,' he said.

'You must look elsewhere for your sustenance, my lord.' Far-Seeing and her children still stared directly up into his face, as if challenging him to attack.

But the Lord of Law crept backwards along the moonbeam road. 'I would be mortal again,' he said. 'What you saw was my mortal self. He still exists. Do you know him? Las Cascadas?' It seemed as if he made a pathetic attempt at familiarity, to win them to his cause through sympathy, but Quelch knew he had failed. 'We shall destroy Chaos and all who serve her.' He glared at Elric and his companion. 'The Singularity shall triumph over Entropy. Death will be checked. We shall abolish Death in all his forms. I am Quelch, a great Lord of Law. You must serve me. It is for the Cause . . .'

Watching him lope away down that long, curving moonbeam road through the multiverse, Elric felt a certain pity for a creature which had abandoned every ideal, every part of its faith, every moral principle, in order to survive for a few more centuries, scavenging off the very souls it claimed to protect.

'What ails that creature, von Bek?'

'They are not immortal but they are almost immortal,' said von Bek. 'The multiverse does not exist in infinity but in quasi-infinity. These are not deliberate paradoxes. Our great archangels fight for control of the Balance. They represent two perfectly reasonable schools of thought and, indeed, are almost the same in habit and belief. Yet they fight – Chaos against Law, Entropy against Stasis – and these arguments are mirrored in all our mortal histories, our daily lives, and are connected in profound but complex ways. Over all this hangs the Cosmic Balance, tilting this way and that but always restoring itself. A wasteful means of maintaining the multiverse, you might say. I think our role is to find less wasteful ways of achieving the same end, to create Order without losing the creativity and fecundity of Chaos. Soon, according to other adepts I have met, there will be a great Conjunction of the multiversal realms, a moment of maximum stability, and it is at this time that the very nature of reality can be changed.'

Elric clapped his hands to his head. 'Sir, I beg you! Cease! I stand here, in the middle of some astral realm, about to tread a moonbeam into near-infinity, and every part of me, physical and spiritual, tells me that I must be irredeemably insane.'

'No,' said Renark von Bek. 'What you behold is the ultimate sanity, the ultimate variety, and perhaps the ultimate order. Come, I will take you home.'

Von Bek turned to the children and addressed Far-Seeing. 'Would you care for a military escort, my lady?'

Her smile was quiet. 'I think I have no further use for swords. Not for the moment. But I thank you, sir.'

Already she was leading her flock away from them, up the steep curve of the moonbeam and into a haze of blue-flecked light. 'I thank you for your song, Prince Elric. For the singing of it you will, in time, be repaid a hundredfold. But I think you will not remember the singing of your song, which brought the Grail to us three, who are, perhaps, its guardians and its beneficiaries. It was the sword which found the Grail and the Grail which led us through. Thank you, sir. You say you are not of the Just, yet I think you are unknowingly of that company. Farewell.'

'Where do you go, Far-Seeing?' asked Melniboné's lord.

'I seek a galaxy they call The Rose, whose planets form one mighty garden. I have seen it in a vision. We shall be the first human creatures to settle it, if it will accept us.'

'I wish you good fortune, my lady,' said Count Renark with a bow.

'And you, sir, as you play the great Game of Time. Good luck to you, also.' Then the child turned her back on them and led her weary flock towards its destiny.

'Can you not see the possibilities?' Von Bek still sought to tempt Elric to his Cause. 'The variety – every curiosity satisfied – and new ones whetted? Friend Elric, I offer you the quasi-infinity of the multiverse, of the First and Second Ethers, and the thrilling life of a trained mukhamir, a player in the great Game.'

'I am a poor gambler, sir.' As if fearing he would not remember them, Elric drank in the wonders all about him: the crowded, constantly swirling, constantly changing multiverse; realm upon realm of reality, most of which knew only the merest hint of the great order in which they played a tiny, but never insignificant, part. He looked down at the misty stuff beneath his feet, which felt as firm as thrice-tempered Imrryrian steel, and he marvelled at the paradoxes, the conflicts of logic. It was almost impossible for his mind to grasp anything but a hint of what this meant. He understood even so that every action taken in the mortal realms was repeated and echoed in the supernatural and vice versa. Every action of every creature in existence had meaning, significance and consequence.

'I once witnessed a fight between archangels and dragons,' von Bek was saying, leading the albino gently down the moonbeam to where it crossed another. 'We will go this way.'

'How do you know where you are? How are time and distance measured here?' Elric was reduced to almost childlike questions. Now he understood what his grimoires had only ever hinted at, unable or unwilling to describe this super-reality. Yet he could not blame his predecessors for their failures. The multiverse defied description. It could, indeed, only be hinted at. There was no language, no logic, no experience which allowed this terrifying and rapturous reality.

'We travel by other means and other instincts,' von Bek assured him. 'If you would join us, you will learn how to navigate not merely the First Ether, but also the Second.'

'You have agreed, Count Renark, to guide me back to my own realm.' Elric was flattered by this strange man's attempts to recruit him.

Von Bek clapped his companion upon the back. 'Fair enough.'

They loped down the moonbeams at a soldier's pace. Elric caught glimpses of worlds, of landscapes, hints of scenes, familiar scents and sounds, completely alien sights, seemingly all at random. For a while he felt his grasp on sanity weakening and, as he walked, the tears streamed down his face. He wept for a loss he could not remember. He wept for the mother he had never known and the father who had refused to know him. He wept for all those who suffered and who would suffer in the useless wars which swept his world and most others. He wept in a mixture of self-pity and a compassion which embraced the multiverse. And then a sense of peace blanketed him.

Stormbringer was still in his hand, unscabbarded. He did not wish to sheathe the blade until the last of that strange Law-light was gone from it. At this moment he understood how the conflict in him between his loyalty to Chaos and his yearning for Law was no simple one and perhaps would never be resolved. Perhaps there was no need to resolve the conflict. Perhaps, however, it could be reconciled.

They walked between the worlds.

They walked for timeless miles, taking this path and then another through the great silver lattice of the moonbeam roads, while everywhere the multiverse blossomed and warped and erupted and glowed, a million worlds in the making, a million realms decaying, and countless billions of mortal souls full of aspiration and despair, and they talked intimately, in low voices, enjoying conversations which only one of them would remember. It seemed sometimes to Elric that he and Count von Bek were the same being, both echoes of some lost original.

And it seemed sometimes that they were free forever of the common bounds of time or space, of pressing human concerns, free to explore the wonderful abstraction of it all, the incredible physicality of this suprareality which they could experience with senses themselves transformed and attuned to the new stimuli. They became reconciled to the notion that little by little their bodies would fade and their spirits blend with the stuff of the multiverse, to find true immortality as a fragment of legend, a hint of a myth, a mark made upon our everlasting cosmic history, which is perhaps the best that most of us will ever know – to have played a part, no matter how small, in that great game, the glorious Game of Time . . .

Many of the company found the tale altogether too fanciful and with rather a strong ecclesiastical bias. At which the conversation turned to metaphysics and, naturally, the company looked to me for my ideas. I was reminded of the time when I first met Edwin Begg and heard his particular story, which is far more familiar, in some aspects, than the one you have just experienced . . .

5. *lunching with the antichrist*

Begg Mansions
Sporting Club Square
London, W14

The Editor
Fulham & Hammersmith Telegraph
Bishops Palace Avenue
London W14

13th October 1992

Sir,

SPIRIT OF THE BLITZ

It is heartening to note, as our economy collapses perhaps for the last time, a return to the language and sentiments of mutual self-interest. London was never the kindest of English cities but of late her cold, self-referential greed has been a watchword around the world. Everything we value is threatened in the name of profit.

I say nothing original when I mourn the fact that it took the Blitz to make Londoners achieve a humanity and heroism they never thought to claim for themselves and which no one expected or demanded of them!

Could we not again aspire to achieve that spirit, without the threat of Hitler but

with the same optimistic courage? Can we
not, in what is surely an hour of need,
marshal what is best in us and find new
means of achieving that justice, equity
and security for which we all long? The
existing methods appear to create as many
victims as they save.

Yours faithfully, Edwin Begg,
former vicar of St Odhran's, Balham.

*HEAR! HEAR! says the Telegraph. This week's Book Token to our
Letter of the Week! Remember, your opinions are important to us
and we want to see them! A £5.00 Book Token for the best!*

My First Encounter With the Clapham Antichrist; His Visions & His Public Career; His Expulsion from the Church & Subsequent Notoriety; His Return to Society & Celebrity as a Sage; His Mysterious & Abrupt Departure Into Hermitage; His Skills in the Kitchen.

'SPIRIT OF THE BLITZ' (a sub-editor's caption) was the last
public statement of the Clapham Antichrist.

Until I read the letter at a friend's I believed Edwin Begg dead some
twenty years ago. The beloved TV eccentric had retired in the 1950s
to live as a recluse in Sporting Club Square, West Kensington. I had
known him intimately in the 60s and 70s and was shocked to learn he
was still alive. I felt a conflicting mixture of emotions, including guilt.
Why had I so readily accepted the hearsay of his death? I wrote to
him at once. Unless he replied to the contrary I would visit him on the
following Wednesday afternoon.

I had met Begg first in 1966 when as a young journalist I interviewed him for a series in the *Star* about London's picturesque

obscurities. Then too I had contacted him after reading one of his letters to the *Telegraph*. The paper, still a substantial local voice, was his only source of news, delivered to him weekly. He refused to have a telephone and communicated mostly through the post.

I had hoped to do a few paragraphs on the Antichrist's career, check a couple of facts with him and obtain a short, preferably amusing, comment on our Fab Sixties. I was delighted when, with cheerful courtesy, Edwin Begg had agreed by return to my request. In a barely legible old-fashioned hand he invited me to lunch.

My story was mostly drafted before I set off to see him. Research had been easy. We had half a filing drawer on Edwin Begg's years of notoriety, first before the War then afterwards as a radio and early TV personality. He had lived in at least a dozen foreign cities. His arguments were discussed in every medium and he became a disputed symbol. Many articles about him were merely sensational, gloating over alleged black magic rites, sexual deviation, miracle-working, blasphemy and sorcery. There were the usual photographs and also drawings, some pretending to realism and others cruel cartoons: the Clapham Antichrist as a monster with blazing eyes and glittering fangs, architect of the doom to come. One showed Hitler, Stalin and Mussolini as his progeny.

The facts were pretty prosaic; in 1931 at the age of 24 Begg was vicar of St Odhran's, Balham, a shabby South London living where few parishioners considered themselves respectable enough to visit a church and were darkly suspicious of those who did. The depression years had almost as many homeless and hungry people on the streets as today. Mosley was gathering a more militant flock than Jesus and those who opposed the Fascists looked to Oxford or the secular left for their moral leadership. Nonetheless the Reverend Begg conscientiously performed his duty, offering the uncertain comforts of his calling to his flock.

Then quite suddenly in 1933 the ordinary hard-working cleric became an urgent proselytiser, an orator. From his late Victorian pulpit he began preaching a shocking message urging Christians to act according to their principles and sacrifice their own material ambitions to the common good, to take a risk on God being right, as he put it. This Tolstoyan exhortation eventually received enough public attention to make his sermons one of London's most popular free attractions from Southwark to Putney, which of course brought him the attention of the famous Bermondsey barrackers, the disapproval of his establishment and the closer interest of the press.

The investigators the Church sent down heard a sermon touching mainly on the current state of the Spanish Republic, how anarchists often acted more like ideal Christians than priests, how people seemed more willing to give their lives to the anarchists than to the cause of Christ. This was reported in *Reynolds News*, tipped off that the investigators would be there, as Begg's urging his congregation to support the coming Antichrist. The report was more or less approving. The disapproving Church investigators, happy for a lead to follow, confirmed the reports. Overnight, the Reverend Edwin Begg, preaching his honest Christian message of brotherly love and equity under the law, became the Clapham Antichrist, Arch Enemy of British Decency, Proud Mocker of All Religion and Hitler's Right Hand, a creature to be driven from our midst.

In the course of a notoriously hasty hearing Edwin Begg was unfrocked, effectively by public demand. In his famous defence Begg confirmed the general opinion of his guilt by challenging the commission to strip itself naked and follow Christ, if they were indeed Christians! He made a disastrous joke: and if they were an example of modern Christians, he said, then after all he probably was the Antichrist!

Begg never returned to his vicarage. He went immediately to Sporting Club Square. Relatives took him in, eventually giving him his own three-roomed flat where it was rumoured he kept a harem of devil-worshipping harlots. The subsequent Siege of Sporting Club Square in which the *News of the World* provoked a riot causing one near-fatality and thousands of pounds worth of damage was over-shadowed by the news of Hitler's massacre of his stormtroopers, the S. A. Goebbels' propaganda became more interesting and rather more in the line of an authentic harbinger of evil, and at last Edwin Begg was left in peace.

Usually attached to a circus or a fair and always billed as 'Reverend' Begg, The Famous Clapham Antichrist! he began to travel the country with his message of universal love. After his first tours he was never a great draw since he disappointed audiences with urgent pleas for sanity and the common good and never rose to the jokes or demands for miracles, but at least he had discovered a way of making a living from his vocation. He spent short periods in prison and there were rumours of a woman in his life, someone he had mentioned early on, though not even the worst of the Sundays found evidence to suggest he was anything but confirmed in his chastity.

When the War came Edwin Begg distinguished himself in the ambulance service, was wounded and decorated. Then he again disappeared from public life. This was his first long period of seclusion in Begg Mansions until suddenly on 1 May, 1949, encouraged by his nephew Robert in BBC Talks, he gave at 9:45 pm on the Home Service the first of his Fireside Observer chats.

No longer the Old Testament boom of the pulpit or the side-show, the Fireside Observer's voice was level, reassuring, humorous, a little sardonic sometimes when referring to authority. He reflected on our continuing hardships and what we might gain through them if we kept trying – what we might expect to see for our children. He offered my parents a vision of a wholesome future worth working for, worth making a few sacrifices for, and they loved him.

He seemed the moral spirit of the Festival of Britain, the best we hoped to become, everything that was decent about being British. An entire book was published proving him the object of a plot in 1934 by a Tory bishop, a Fascist sympathiser, and there were dozens of articles, newsreels and talks describing him as the victim of a vicious hoax or showing how Mosley had needed a scapegoat.

Begg snubbed the Church's willingness to review his case in the light of his new public approval and continued to broadcast the reassuring ironies which lightened our 1950s darkness and helped us create the golden years of the 1960s and 70s. He did not believe his dream to be illusory.

By 1950 he was on television, part of the *Thinkers' Club* with Gilbert Harding and Professor Joad, which every week discussed an important contemporary issue. The programme received the accolade of being lampooned in *Radio Fun* as *The Stinkers' Club* with Headwind Legg which happened to be one of my own childhood favourites. He appeared, an amiable sage, on panel games, quiz shows, programmes called *A Crisis of Faith* or *Turning Point* and at religious conferences eagerly displaying their tolerance by soliciting the opinion of a redeemed antichrist.

Suddenly, in 1955, Begg refused to renew all broadcasting contracts and retired from public life, first to travel and finally to settle back in Begg Mansions with his books and his journals. He never explained his decision and then the public lost interest. New men with brisker messages were bustling in to build Utopia for us in our lifetime.

Contenting himself with a few letters mostly on parochial matters to the Hammersmith *Telegraph*, Edwin Begg lived undisturbed for a decade. His works of popular philosophy sold steadily until British fashion changed. Writing nothing after 1955, he encouraged his books to go out of print. He kept his disciples, of course, who sought his material in increasingly obscure places and wrote to him concerning his uncanny understanding of their deepest feelings, the ways in which he had dramatically changed their lives, and to whom, it was reported, he never replied.

The first Wednesday I took the 28 from Notting Hill Gate down North Star Road to Greyhound Gardens. I had brought my A-Z. I had never been to Sporting Club Square before and was baffled by the surrounding network of tiny twisting streets, none of which seemed to go in the same direction for more than a few blocks, the result of frenzied rival building work during the speculative 1880s when developers had failed to follow the plans agreed between themselves, the freeholder, the architect and the authorities. The consequent recession ensured that nothing was ever done to remedy the mess. Half-finished crescents and abrupt culs-de-sac, odd patches of wasteland, complicated rights of way involving narrow alleys, walls, gates and ancient pathways were interrupted, where bomb damage allowed, by the new council estates, totems of clean enlightenment geometry whose erection would automatically cause all surrounding social evils to wither away. I had not expected to find anything quite so depressing and began to feel sorry for Begg ending his days in such circumstances, but turning out of Margrave Passage I came suddenly upon a cluster of big unkempt oaks and cedars gathered about beautiful wrought-iron gates in the baroque oriental regency style of Old Cogges, that riot of unnatural ruin, the rural seat of the Beggs which William the Goth remodelled in 1798 to rival Strawberry Hill. They were miraculous in the early afternoon sun: the gates to paradise.

The Square now has a preservation order and appears in international books of architecture as the finest example of its kind. Sir Hubert Begg, its architect, is mentioned in the same breath as Gaudi and Norman Shaw, which will give you some notion of his peculiar talent. Inspired by the fluid aesthetics of the fin-de-siècle he was loyal to his native brick and fired almost every fancy from Buckingham clay to give his vast array of disparate styles an inexplicable coherence. The tennis courts bear the motifs of some Mucha-influenced smith, their floral metalwork garlanded with living roses and honeysuckle from spring until autumn: even the benches are on record as one of the loveliest expressions of public art nouveau.

Until 1960 there had been a black chain across the Square's entrance and a porter on duty day and night. Residents' cars were never seen in the road but garaged in the little William Morris cottages originally designed as studios and running behind the eccentrically magnificent palaces, which had been Begg's Folly until they survived the Blitz to become part of our heritage. When I walked up to the gates in 1966 a few cars had appeared in the gravel road running around gardens enclosed by other leafy ironwork after Charles Rennie Mackintosh, and the Square had a bit of a shamefaced seedy appearance.

There were only a few uniformed porters on part-time duty by then and they too had a slightly hangdog air. The Square was weathering one of its periodic declines, having again failed to connect with South Kensington during a decade of prosperity. Only the bohemian middle classes were actually proud to live there, so the place had filled with actors, music hall performers, musicians, singers, writers, cheque-kiters and artists of every kind, together with journalists, designers and retired dance instructresses, hairdressers and disappointed legatees muttering bitterly about any blood not their own, for the Square had taken refugees and immigrants. Others came to be near the tennis courts maintained by the SCS Club affiliated to nearby Queen's.

Several professionals had taken apartments in Wratislaw Villas, so the courts never went down and neither did the gardens which were preserved by an endowment from Gordon Begg, Lord Mauleverer, the botanist and explorer, whose elegant vivarium still pushed its flaking white girders and steamy glass above exotic shrubbery near the Mandrake Road entrance. Other examples of his botanical treasures, the rival of Holland's, flourished here and there about the Square and now feathery exotics mingled with the oaks and hawthorn of the original Saxon meadow.

Arriving in this unexpected tranquillity on a warm September afternoon when the dramatic red sun gave vivid contrast to the terracotta, the deep greens of trees, lawns and shrubbery, I paused in astonished delight. Dreamily I continued around the Square in the direction shown me by the gatehouse porter. I was of a generation which enthused over pre-Raphaelite paint and made Beardsley its own again, who had bought the five shilling Mackintosh chairs and sixpenny Muchas and ten bob Lalique glass in Portobello Road to decorate Liberty-oriental pads whose fragrant patchouli never disguised the pungent dope. They were the best exmaples we could find in this world to remind us of what we had seen on our acid voyages.

To my father's generation the Square would be unspeakably old-fashioned, redolent of the worst suburban pretension, but I had come upon a gorgeous secret. I understood why so few people mentioned it, how almost everyone was either enchanted or repelled. My contemporaries, who thought 'Georgian' the absolute height of excellence and imposed their stern developments upon Kensington's levelled memory, found Sporting Club Square hideously 'Victorian' – a gigantic, grubby whatnot. Others dreamed of the day when they would have the power to be free of Sporting Club Square, the power to raze her and raise their fake Le Corbusier mile-high concrete in triumph above the West London brick.

I did not know, as I made my way past great mansions of Caligari Tudor and Kremlin De Mille, that I was privileged to find the Square in the final years of her glory. In those days I enjoyed a wonderful innocence and could no more visualise this lovely old place changing for the worse than I could imagine the destruction of Dubrovnik.

Obscured, sometimes, by her trees, the mansion apartments of Sporting Club Square revealed a thousand surprises. I was in danger of being late as I stared at Rossettian gargoyles and Blakean cary-atids, copings, gables, corbels of every possible stamp yet all bearing the distinctive style of their time. I was filled with an obscure sense of epiphany.

In 1886, asymmetrical Begg Mansions was the boldest expression of modernism, built by the architect for his own family use, for his offices and studios, his living quarters, a suite to entertain clients, and to display his designs, accommodation for his draughts- and crafts-people whose studios in attics and basements produced the prototype glass, metal, furniture and fabrics which nowadays form the basis of the V&A's extraordinary collection. By the 1920s after Hubert Begg's death the Square became unfashionable. Lady Begg moved to Holland Park and Begg Mansions filled up with the poorer Beggs who paid only the communal fee for general upkeep and agreed to main-tain their own flats in good condition. Their acknowledged patron was old Squire Begg, who had the penthouse. By 1966 the building was a labyrinth of oddly twisting corridors and stairways, unexpected landings reached by two old oak and copper cage elevators served by their own generator, which worked on an eccentric system devised by the architect and was always going wrong. Later I learned that it was more prudent to walk the six flights to Edwin Begg's rooms but on that first visit I got into the lift, pressed the stud for the sixth floor and was taken up without incident in a shower of sparks and rattling brass to the ill-lit landing where the Antichrist himself awaited me.

I recognised him of course but was surprised that he seemed healthier than I had expected. He was a little plumper and his bone-white hair was cropped in a self-administered pudding-basin cut. He was clean shaven, pink and bright as a mouse, with startling blue eyes, a firm rather feminine mouth and the long sharp nose of his mother's Lowland Presbyterian forefathers. His high voice had an old-fashioned Edwardian elegance and was habitually rather measured. He reminded me of a Wildean *grande-dame*, tiny but imposing. I was dressed like most of my Ladbroke Grove peers and he seemed pleased by my appearance, offering me his delicate hand, introducing himself and muttering about my good luck with the lift. He had agreed to this interview, he said, because he'd been feeling unusually optimistic after playing the new Beatles album. We shared our enthusiasm.

He guided me back through those almost organic passages until we approached his flat and a smell so heady, so delicious that I did not at first identify it as food. His front door let directly onto his study which led to a sitting room and bedroom. Only the dining room seemed unchanged since 1900 and still had the original Voysey wallpaper and furniture, a Henry dresser and Benson copperware. Like many reclusive people he enjoyed talking. As he continued to cook he sat me on a sturdy Wilson stool with a glass of wine and asked me about my career, showing keen interest in my answers.

'I hope you don't mind home cooking,' he said. 'It's a habit I cultivated when I lived on the road. Is there anything you find disagreeable to eat?'

I would have eaten strychnine if it had tasted as that first meal tasted. We had mysterious sauces whose nuances I can still recall, wines of exquisite delicacy, a dessert which contained an entire orchestra of flavours, all prepared in his tiny perfect 1920s 'modern' kitchenette to one side of the dining room.

After we had eaten he suggested we take our coffee into the bed-room to sit in big wicker chairs and enjoy another wonderful revelation. He drew the curtains back from his great bay window to reveal over two miles of almost unbroken landscape all the way to the river with the spires and roofs of Old Putney beyond. In the far distance was a familiar London skyline but immediately before us were the Square's half-wild communal gardens and cottage garages, then the ivy-covered walls of St Mary's Convent, the Convent School sports field and that great forest of shrubs, trees and memorial sculptures, the West London Necropolis, whose Victorian angels raised hopeful swords against the ever-changing sky. Beyond the cemetery was the steeple of St Swithold's and her churchyard, then a nurtured patch-work of allotments, some old alms cottages and finally the sturdy topiary of the Bishop's Gardens surrounding a distant palace whose

Tudor dignity did much to inspire Hubert Begg. The formal hedges marched all the way to the bird sanctuary on a broad, marshy curve where the Thames approached Hammersmith Bridge, a medieval fantasy.

It was the pastoral and monumental in perfect harmony which some cities spontaneously create. Edwin Begg said the landscape was an unfailing inspiration. He could dream of Roman galleys beating up the river cautiously alert for Celtic war-parties or Vikings striking at the Bishop's Palace leaving flames and murder behind. He liked to think of other more contemplative eyes looking on a landscape scarcely changed in centuries. 'Hogarth, Turner and Whistler amongst them. Wheldrake, writing *Harry Wharton*, looked out from this site when staying at the Sporting Club Tavern and earlier Augusta Begg conceived the whole of *The Bravo of Bohemia* and most of *Yamboo; or, The North American Slave* while seated more or less where I am now! Before he went off to become an orientalist and London's leading painter of discreet seraglios James Lewis Porter painted several large landscapes which show market gardens where the allotments are, a few more cottages, but not much else has changed. I can walk downstairs, out of the back door, through that gate, cross the convent field into the graveyard, take the path through the church down to the allotments all the way to the Bishop's Gardens and be at the bird sanctuary within half-an-hour, even cross the bridge into Putney and the Heath if I feel like it and hardly see a house, a car or another human being!' He would always stop for a bun, he said, at the old Palace Tea Rooms and usually strolled back via Margrave Avenue's interesting junkyards. Mrs White, who kept the best used bookshop there, told me he came in at least twice a week.

He loved to wake up before dawn with his curtains drawn open and watch the sun gradually reveal familiar sights. 'No small miracle, these days, dear! I'm always afraid that one morning it won't be there.' At the time I thought this no more than a mildly philosophical remark.

For me he still had the aura of a mythic figure from my childhood, someone my parents had revered. I was prepared to dislike him but was immediately charmed by his gentle eccentricity, his rather loud plaid shirts and corduroys, his amiable vagueness. The quality of the lunch alone would have convinced me of his virtue!

I was of the 1960s, typically idealistic and opinionated and probably pretty obnoxious to him but he saw something he liked about me and I fell in love with him. He was my ideal father.

I returned home to rewrite my piece. A figure of enormous wisdom, he offered practical common sense, I said, in a world ruled by the abstract sophistries and empty reassurances heralding the new spirit of competition into British society. It was the only piece of mine the *Star* never used, but on that first afternoon Edwin Begg invited me back for lunch and on almost every Wednesday for the next eight years, even after I married, I would take the 28 from the Odeon, Westbourne Grove to Greyhound Gardens and walk through alleys of stained concrete, past shabby red terraces and doorways stinking of rot until I turned that corner and stood again before the magnificent gates of Sporting Club Square.

My friend kept his curiosity about me and I remained flattered by his interest. He was always fascinating company, whether expanding on some moral theme or telling a funny story. One of his closest chums had been Harry Lupino Begg, the music hall star, and he had also known Al Bowlly. He was a superb and infectious mimic and could reproduce Lupino's patter by heart, making it as topical and fresh as the moment. His imitation of Bowlly singing 'Buddy, Can You Spare a Dime' was uncanny. When carried away by some amusing story or conceit his voice would rise and fall in rapid and entertaining profusion, sometimes taking on a birdlike quality difficult to follow. In the main however he spoke with the deliberate air of one who respected the effect of words upon the world.

By his own admission the Clapham Antichrist was not a great original thinker but he spoke from original experience. He helped me look again at the roots of my beliefs. Through him I came to understand the innocent intellectual excitement of the years before political experiments turned one by one into tyrannical orthodoxies. He loaned me my first Kropotkin, the touching *Memoirs of an Anarchist*, and helped me understand the difference between moral outrage and social effect. He loved works of popular intellectualism. He was as great an enthusiast for Huxley's *The Perennial Philosophy* as he was for Winwood Reade's boisterously secular *Martyrdom of Man*. He introduced me to the interesting late work of H G Wells and to Elizabeth Bowen. He led me to an enjoyment of Jane Austen I had never known. He infected me with his enthusiasm for the more obscure Victorians who remained part of his own living library and he was generous with his books. But, no matter how magical our afternoons, he insisted I must always be gone before the BBC broadcast Choral Evensong. Only in the dead of winter did I ever leave Sporting Club Square in darkness.

Naturally I was curious to know why he had retired so abruptly from public life. Had he told the church of his visions? Why had he felt such an urgent need to preach? To risk so much public disapproval? Eventually I asked him how badly it had hurt him to be branded as the premier agent of the Great Antagonist, the yapping dog as it were at the heels of the Son of the Morning. He said he had retreated from the insults before they had grown unbearable. 'But it wasn't difficult to snub people who asked you questions like "Tell me, Mr Begg, what does human blood taste like?" Besides, I had my Rose to sustain me, my vision . . .'

I hoped he would expand on this but he only chuckled over some. association he had made with an obscure temptation of St Anthony and then asked me if I had been to see his cousin Orlando Begg's *Flaming Venus*, now on permanent display at the Tate.

Though I was soon addicted to his company, I always saw him on the same day and time every week. As he grew more comfortable with me he recounted the history of his family and Sporting Club Square. He spoke of his experiences as a young curate, as a circus entertainer, as a television personality, and he always cooked. This was, he said, the one time he indulged his gourmet instincts. In the summer we would stroll in the gardens or look at the tennis matches. Sitting on benches we would watch the birds or the children playing. When I asked him questions about his own life his answers became fuller, though never completely unguarded.

It was easy to see how in his determined naïveté he was once in such frequent conflict with authority.

'I remember saying, my dear, to the magistrate— Who does not admire the free-running, intelligent fox? And few, no matter how inconvenienced, begrudge him his prey which is won by daring raiding and quick wits, risking all. A bandit, your honour, one can admire and prepare against. There is even a stirring or two of romance for the brigand chief. But once the brigand becomes a baron that's where the balance goes wrong, eh, your honour? It gets unfair, I said to him. Our sympathies recognise these differences so why can't our laws? Our courts make us performers in pieces of simplistic fiction! Why do we continue to waste so much time? The magistrate said he found my last remark amusing and gave me the maximum sentence.'

Part of Edwin Begg's authority came from his vivacity. As he sat across from me at the table, putting little pieces of chicken into his mouth, pausing to enjoy them, then launching off onto a quite different subject, he seemed determined to relish every experience, every moment. His manner offered a clue to his past. Could he be so entertaining because he might otherwise have to confront an unpleasant truth? Anyone raised in a post-Freudian world could make that guess. But it was not necessarily correct.

Sometimes his bright eyes would dart away to a picture or glance through a window and I learned to interpret this fleeting expression as one of pain or sadness. He admitted readily that he had retreated into his inner life, feeling he had failed in both his public and private missions. I frequently reassured him of his value, the esteem in which he was still held, but he was unconvinced.

'Life isn't a matter of linear consequences,' he said. 'We only try to make it look like that. Our job is not to force grids upon the world but to achieve harmony with nature.'

At that time in my life such phrases made me reach for my hat, if not my revolver, but because I loved him so much I tried to understand what he meant. He believed that in our terror we imposed perverse linearity upon a naturally turbulent universe, that our perceptions of time were at fault since we saw the swirling cosmos as still or slow-moving just as a gnat doubtless sees us. He thought that those who overcame their brute terror of the truth soon attained the state of the angels.

The Clapham Antichrist was disappointed that I was not more sympathetic to the mystical aspects of the alternative society but because of my familiarity with its ideas was glad to have me for a devil's advocate. I was looking for a fast road to Utopia and he had almost given up finding any road at all. Our solutions were wrong because our analysis was wrong, he said. We needed to rethink our fundamental principles and find better means of applying them. I argued that this would take too long. Social problems required urgent action. His attitude was an excuse for inaction. In the right hands there was nothing wrong with the existing tools.

'And what are the right hands, dear?' he asked. 'Who makes the rules? Who keeps them, my dear?' He ran his thin fingers through hair which became a milky halo around his earnest face. 'And how is it possible to make them and keep them when our logic insists on such oppressive linearity? We took opium into China and bled them of their silver. Now they send heroin to us to lay hands upon our currency! Am I the only one enjoying the irony? The Indians are reclaiming the Southwestern United States in a massive migration back into the old French and Spanish lands. The world is never still, is it, my dear?'

*

His alert features were full of tiny signals, humorous and anxious, enquiring and defiant, as he expanded on his philosophy one autumn afternoon. We strolled around the outer path enjoying the late roses and early chrysanthemums forming an archway roofed with fading honeysuckle. He wore his green raglan, his yellow scarf, his hideous turf accountant's trilby, and gestured with the blackthorn he always carried but hardly used. 'The world is never still and yet we continue to live as if turbulence were not the natural order of things. We have no more attained our ultimate state than has our own star! We have scarcely glimpsed any more of the multiverse than a toad under a stone! We are part of the turbulence and it is in turbulence we thrive. Once that's understood, my dear, the rest is surely easy? Brute warfare is our crudest expression of natural turbulence, our least productive. What's the finest? Surely there's no evil in aspiring to be our best? What do we gain by tolerating or even justifying the worst?'

I sat down on the bench looking the length of a bower whose pale golds and browns were given a tawny burnish by the sun. Beyond the hedges was the sound of a tennis game. 'And those were the ideas which so offended the Church?' I asked.

He chuckled, his face sharp with self mockery. 'Not really. They had certain grounds I suppose. I don't know. I merely suggested to my congregation after the newspapers had begun the debate, that perhaps only through Chaos and Anarchy could the Millennium be achieved. There were after all certain clues to that effect in the Bible. I scarcely think I'm to blame if this was interpreted as calling for bloody revolution, or heralding Armageddon and the Age of the Antichrist!'

I was diplomatic. 'Perhaps you made the mistake of overestimating your audiences?'

Smiling he turned where he sat to offer me a reproving eye. 'I did not overestimate them, my dear. They underestimated themselves. They didn't appreciate that I was trying to help them become one with the angels. I have experienced such miracles, my dear! Such wonderful visions!'

And then quite suddenly he had risen and taken me by my arm to the Duke's Elm, the ancient tree which marked the border of the larger square in what was really a cruciform. Beyond the elm were lawns and well-stocked beds of the cross's western bar laid out exactly as Begg had planned. Various residents had brought their deckchairs here to enjoy the last of the summer. There was a leisurely good-humoured holiday air to the day. It was then, quite casually and careless of passers-by, that the Clapham Antichrist described to me the vision which converted him from a mild-mannered Anglican cleric into a national myth.

'It was on a similar evening to this in 1933. Hitler had just taken power. I was staying with my Aunt Constance Cunningham, the actress, who had a flat in D'Yss Mansions and refused to associate with the other Beggs. I had come out here for a stroll to smoke my pipe and think over a few ideas for the next Sunday's sermon which I would deliver, my dear, to a congregation consisting mostly of the miserably senile and the irredeemably small-minded who came to church primarily as a signal to neighbours they believed beneath them . . .

'It was a bloody miserable prospect. I have since played better audiences on a wet Thursday night in a ploughed field outside Leeds. No matter what happened to me I never regretted leaving those dour ungiving faces behind. I did my best. My sermons were intended to discover the smallest flame of charity and aspiration burning in their tight little chests. I say all this in sad retrospect. At the time I was wrestling with my refusal to recognise certain truths and find a faith not threatened by them.

'I really was doing my best, my dear.' He sighed and looked upward through the lattice of branches at the jackdaw nests just visible amongst the fading leaves. 'I was quite agitated about my failure to discover a theme appropriate to their lives. I wouldn't give in to temptation and concentrate on the few decent parishioners at the expense of the rest.' He turned to look across the lawns at the romantic rococo splendour of Moreau Mansions. 'It was a misty evening in the Square with the sun setting through those big trees over there, a hint of pale gold in the haze and bold comforting shadows on the grass. I stood here, my dear, by the Duke's Elm. There was nobody else around. My vision stepped forward, out of the mist, and smiled at me.

'At first I thought that in my tiredness I was hallucinating. I'd been trained to doubt any ecstatic experience. The scent of roses was intense, like a drug! Could this be Carterton's ghost said to haunt the spot where he fell to his death, fighting a duel in the branches after a drunken night at Begg's? But this was no young duke. The woman was about my own height, with graceful beauty and the air of peace I associated with the Virgin. My unconventional madonna stood in a mannish confident way, a hand on her hip, clearly amused by me. She appeared to have emerged from the earth or from the tree. Shadows of bark and leaves still clung to her. There was something plant-like about the set of her limbs, the subtle colours of her flesh, as if a rose had become human and yet remained thoroughly a rose. I was rather frightened at first, my dear.

'I'd grown up with an Anglicanism permitting hardly a hint of the Pit, so I didn't perceive her as a temptress. I was thoroughly aware of her sexuality and in no way threatened by it or by her vitality. After a moment the fear dissipated, then after a few minutes she vanished and I was left with what I could only describe as her inspiration which led me to write my first real sermon that evening and present it on the following Sunday.'

'She gave you a message?' I thought of Jeanne D'Arc.

'Oh, no. Our exchange was wordless on that occasion.'

'And you spoke of her in church?'

'Never. That would have been a sort of betrayal. No, I based my message simply on the emotion she had aroused in me. A vision of Christ might have done the same. I don't know.'

'So it was a Christian message? Not anti-Christian?'

'Not anti-religious, at any rate. Perhaps, as the bishop suggested, a little pagan.'

'What brought you so much attention?'

'In the church that Sunday were two young chaps escorting their recently widowed aunt, Mrs Nye. They told their friends about me. To my delight when I gave my second sermon I found myself with a very receptive congregation. I thanked God for the miracle. It seemed nothing else, my dear. You can't imagine the joy of it! For any chap in my position. I'd received a gift of divine communication, perhaps a small one, but it seemed pretty authentic. And the people began to pack St Odhran's. We had money for repairs. They seemed so willing suddenly to give themselves to their faith!'

I was mildly disappointed. This Rose did not seem much of a vision. Under the influence of drugs or when overtired I had experienced hallucinations quite as elaborate and inspiring. I asked him if he had seen her again.

'Oh, yes. Of course. Many times. In the end we fell in love. She taught me so much. Later there was a child.'

He stood up, adjusted his overcoat and scarf and gave his stick a little flourish. He pointed out how the light fell through the parade of black gnarled maples leading to the tennis courts. 'An army of old giants ready to march,' he said. 'But their roots won't let them.'

The next Wednesday when I came to lunch he said no more about his vision.

CHAPTER TWO

A Brief History of the Begg Family
& of Sporting Club Square

In the course of my first four hundred lunches with the Clapham Antichrist I never did discover why he abandoned his career but I learned a great deal about the Begg family, its origins, its connections and its property, especially the Square. I became something of an expert and planned a monograph until the recent publication of two excellent Hubert Begg books made my work only useful as an appendix to real scholarship.

Today the Square, on several tourist itineraries, has lost most traces of its old unselfconscious integrity. Only Begg Mansions remains gated and fenced from casual view, a defiantly private museum of human curiosities. The rest of the Square has been encouraged to maximise its profitability. Bakunin Villas is now the Hotel Romanoff. Ralph Lauren for some time sponsored D'Yss Mansions as a fashion gallery. Beardsley Villas is let as company flats to United Foods, while the council (which invested heavily in BBIC) took another building, the Moorish fantasy of Flecker Mansions, as offices. There is still some talk of an international company 'theme-parking' Sporting Club Square, running commercial tennis matches and linking it to a television soap. Following the financial scandals involving Begg Belgravia International and its associate companies, the Residents' Association has had some recent success in reversing this progress.

When I visited Edwin Begg in 1992, he welcomed me as if our routine had never been broken. He mourned his home's decline into a mere fashion, an exploitable commodity instead of a respected eccentricity, and felt it had gone the way of the Chateau Pantin or Derry & Toms famous Roof Garden, with every feature displayed as an emphatic curiosity, a sensation, a mode, and all her old charm a wistful memory. He had early on warned them about these likely consequences of his nephew's eager speculations. 'Barbican wasn't the first to discover what you could do in a boom economy with a lick of paint, but I thought his soiling of his own nest a remote chance, not one of his first moves! The plans of such people are generally far advanced before they achieve power. When they strike you are almost always taken unawares, aren't you, dear? What cold, patient dreams they must have.'

He derived no satisfaction from Barbican Begg's somewhat ignoble ruin but felt deep sympathy for his fellow residents hopelessly trying to recover their stolen past.

'It's too late for us now and soon it won't matter much, but it's hard to imagine the kind of appetite which feeds upon souls like locusts on corn. We might yet drive the locust from our field, my dear, but he has already eaten his fill. He has taken what we cannot replace.'

Sometimes he was a little difficult to follow and his similes grew increasingly bucolic.

'The world's changing physically, dear. Can't you feel it?' His eyes were as bright a blue and clear as always, his pink cheeks a little more drawn, his white halo thinner, but he still pecked at the middle-distance when he got excited, as if he could tear the truth from the air with his nose. He was clearly delighted that we had resumed our meetings. He apologised that the snacks were things he could make and microwave. They were still delicious. On our first meeting I was close to tears, wondering why on earth I had simply assumed him dead and deprived myself of his company for so long. He suggested a stroll if I could stand it.

I admitted that the Square was not improving. I had been appalled at the gaudy golds and purples of the Hotel Romanoff. It was, he said, currently in receivership, and he shrugged. 'What is it, my dear, which allows us to become the victims of such villains, time after time! Time after time they take what is best in us and turn it to our disadvantage. It's like being a conspirator in one's own rape.'

We had come up to the Duke's Elm again in the winter twilight and he spoke fondly of familiar ancestors.

Cornelius van Beek, a Dutch cousin of the Saxon von Beks, had settled in London in 1689, shortly after William and Mary. For many Europeans in those days England was a haven of relative enlighten-ment. A daring merchant banker, van Beek financed exploratory trading expeditions, accompanying several of them himself, and amassed the honourable fortune enabling him to retire at sixty to Cogges Hall, Sussex. Amongst his properties when he died were the North Star Farm and tavern, west of Kensington, bought on the mistaken assumption that the area was growing more respectable and where he had at one time planned to build a house. This notorious stretch of heath was left to van Beek's nephew, George Arthur Begg who had anglicised his name upon marriage to Harriet Vernon, his second cousin, in 1738. Their only surviving grandson was Robert Vernon Begg, famous as Dandy Bob Begg and ennobled under the Prince Regent.

As financially impecunious as his patron, Dandy Bob raised money from co-members of the Hellfire, took over the old tavern at North Star Farm, increased its size and magnificence, entertained the picaro captains so they would go elsewhere for their prizes, ran bare-knuckle fights, bear-baitings and other brutal spectacles, and founded the most notorious sporting establishment of its day. Fortunes were commonly lost and won at Begg's; suicides, scandals and duels no rarity. A dozen of our oldest families spilled their blood in the meadow beneath the black elm, and perhaps a score of men and women drowned in the brook now covered and serving as a modern sewer.

Begg's Sporting Club grew so infamous, the activities of its members and their concubines such a public outrage, that when the next William ascended, Begg rapidly declined. By Victoria's crowning the great dandy whom all had courted had become a souse married into the Wadhams for their money, got his wife Charlotte pregnant with male twins and died, whereupon she somewhat boldly married his nephew Captain Russell Begg and had three more children before he died a hero and a colonel in the Crimea. The twins were Ernest Sumara and Louis Palmate Begg, her two girls were Adriana Circe and Juliana Aphrodite and her youngest boy, her favourite child, was Hubert Alhambra born on January 18th 1855 after his father's fatal fall at Balaclava.

A youthful disciple of Eastlake, by the late 1870s Hubert Begg was a practising architect whose largest single commission was Castle Bothwell on the shores of Loch Ness (his sister had married James Bothwell) which became a victim of the Glasgow blitz. 'But it was little more than a bit of quasi-Eastlake and no rival for instance to the V&A,' Edwin Begg had told me. He did not share my admiration for his great-uncle's achievement. 'Quite frankly, his best work was always his furniture.' He was proud of his complete bedroom suite in Begg's rather spare late style but he did not delight in living in 'an art nouveau wedding cake'. He claimed the Square's buildings cost up to ten times as much to clean as Oakwood Mansions, for instance, at the western end of Kensington High Street. 'Because of the crannies and fancy mouldings, those flowing fauns and smirking sylphs the late Victorians found so deliciously sexy. Dust traps all. It's certainly unique, my dear, but so was Quasimodo.'

*

Hubert Begg never struggled for a living. He had married the beautiful Carinthia Hughes, an American heiress, during his two years in Baltimore and it was she who suggested he use family land for his own creation, tearing down that ramshackle old firetrap, The Sporting Club Tavern, which together with a smallholding was rented to a family called Foulsham whom Begg generously resettled on prime land, complete with their children, their cow, their pig and various other domestic animals, near Old Cogges.

The North Star land was cleared. North Star Square was named but lasted briefly as that. It was designed as a true square with four other smaller squares around it to form a sturdy box cross, thus allowing a more flexible way of arranging the buildings, ensuring residents plenty of light, good views and more tennis. Originally there were plans for seven tennis courts. By the 1880s tennis was a social madness rather than a vogue and everybody was playing. Nearby Queens Club was founded in Begg's shadow. Begg's plans were altogether more magnificent and soon the projected settlement blossomed into Sporting Club Square. The name had a slightly raffish, romantic reference and attracted the more daring young people, the financiers who still saw themselves as athletic privateers and who were already patrons to an artist or two as a matter of form.

Clients were encouraged to commission favourite styles for Begg to adapt. He had already turned his back on earlier influences, so Gothic did not predominate, but was well represented in Lohengrin Villas which was almost an homage to Eastlake, commissioned by the Church to house retired clergy who felt comfortable with its soaring arches and mighty buttresses. Encouraged by the enthusiasm for his scheme, the architect was able to indulge every fantasy, rather in the manner of a precocious Elgar offering adaptations of what Greaves called, in *The British Architect*, 'Mediterranean, Oriental, Historical and Modern styles representing the quintessence of contemporary taste.' But there were some who even then found it fussy and decadent. When the queen praised it as an example to the world Begg was knighted. Lady Carinthia, who survived him by many years, always credited herself as the Square's real procreator and it must be said it was she who nudged her husband away from the past to embrace a more plastic future.

Work on Sporting Club Square began in 1885 but was not entirely completed until 1901. The slump of the 1890s destroyed the aspirations of the rising bourgeoisie, who were to have been the likely renters; Gibbs and Flew had bankrupted themselves building the Olympia Bridge, and nobody who still had money felt secure enough to cross into the new suburbs. Their dreams of elevation now frustrated, the failed and dispossessed took their new bitter poverty with them into the depths of a North Star development doomed never to rise and to become almost at once a watchword for social decrepitude, populated by loafers, psychopaths, unstable landladies, exploited seamstresses, drunkards, forgers, beaten wives, braggarts, embezzlers, rat-faced children, petty officials and prostitutes who had grown accustomed to the easy prosperity of the previous decade and were now deeply resentful of anyone more fortunate. They swiftly turned the district into everything it remained until the next tide of prosperity lifted it for a while, only to let it fall back almost in relief as another generation lost its hold upon life's ambitions. The terraces were occupied by casual labourers and petty thieves while the impoverished petite bourgeoisie sought the mews and parades. North Star became a synonym for wretchedness and miserable criminality and was usually avoided even by the police.

By 1935 the area was a warren to rival Notting Dale, but Sporting Club Square, the adjoining St Mary's Convent and the churchyard, retained a rather dreamy, innocent air, untouched by the prevailing mood. Indeed locals almost revered and protected the Square's tranquillity as if it were the only thing they had ever held holy and were proud of it. During the last war the Square was untouched by incendiaries roaring all around, but some of the flats were already abandoned and then taken over by the government to house mostly Jewish political exiles and these added to the cosmopolitan atmosphere. For years a Polish delicatessen stood on the corner of North Star Road; it was possible to buy all kinds of kosher food at Mrs Green's grocery, Mandrake Terrace, and the Foulsham Road French patisserie remained popular until 1980 when Madame Stejns retired. According to Edwin Begg, the War and the years of austerity were their best, with a marvellous spirit of cooperation everywhere. During the War and until 1954 open air concerts were regularly performed by local musicians and an excellent theatrical group was eventually absorbed into the Lyric until that was rationalised. A song, *The Rose of Sporting Club Square*, was popular in the 1930s and the musical play it was written for was the basis of a Hollywood musical in 1940. The David Glazier Ensemble, perhaps the most innovative modern dance troupe of its day, occupied all the lower flats in Le Gallienne Chambers.

Edwin Begg was not the only resident to become famous with the general public. Wheldrake's association with the old tavern, where he spent two years of exile, is well known. Audrey Vernon lived most of her short life in Dowson Mansions. Her lover, Warwick Harden, took a flat in Ibsen Studios next door and had a door built directly through to her bedroom. John Angus Gilchrist the mass murderer lived here but dispatched his nearest victim three miles away in Shepherd's Bush. Others associated with the Square, sometimes briefly, included W Pett Ridge, George Robey, Gustav Klimt, Rebecca West, Constance Cummings, Jessie Matthews, Sonny Hale, Jack Parker, Gerald Kersh, Laura Riding, Joseph Kiss, John Lodwick, Edith Sitwell, Lord George Creech, Angela Thirkell, G K Chesterton, Max Miller, Sir Compton Mackenzie, Margery Allingham, Ralph Richardson, Eudora Welty, Donald Peers, Max Wall, Dame Fay Westbrook, Graham Greene, Eduardo Paolozzi, Gore Vidal, Bill Butler, Jimi Hendrix, Jack Trevor Story, Laura Ashley, Mario Amayo, Angela Carter, Simon Russell Beale, Ian Dury, Jonathan Carroll and a variety of sports and media personalities. As its preserves were stripped, repackaged and sold off during the feeding frenzy of the 1980s only the most stubborn residents refused to be driven from the little holdings they had once believed their birthright, but it was not until Edwin Begg led me back to his bedroom and raised the newly-installed blind that I understood the full effect of his nephew's speculations. 'We do not rest, do we,' he said, 'from mortal toil? But I'm not sure this is my idea of the new Jerusalem. What do you think, dear?'

They had taken his view, all that harmony. I was consumed with a sense of unspeakable outrage! They had turned that beautiful land-scape into a muddy wasteland in which it seemed some monstrous, petulant child had scattered at random its filthy Tonka trucks and Corgi cranes, Portakabins, bulldozers in crazed abandon, then in tan-trum stepped on everything. That perfect balance was destroyed and the tranquillity of Sporting Club Square was now forever under siege. The convent was gone, as well as the church.

'I read in the *Telegraph* that it required the passage of two private member's bills, the defiance of several preservation orders, the bribery of officials in thirteen different government departments and the blackmailing of a cabinet minister just to annex a third of the cem-etery and knock down the chapel and almshouses,' Begg said.

Meanwhile the small fry had looted the cemetery of its saleable masonry. Every monument had been chiselled. The severed heads of the angels were already being sold in the antique boutiques of Mayfair and St Germaine-des-Prés. Disappointed in their share of this loot, others had daubed swastikas and obscenities on the remaining stones.

'It's private building land now,' said Begg. 'They have dogs and fences. They bulldozered St Swithold's. You can't get to the Necropolis, let alone the river. Still, this is probably better than what they were going to build.'

The activities of Barbican Begg and his associates, whose enterprises claimed more victims than Maxwell, have been discussed everywhere, but one of the consequences of BBIC's speculations was that bleak no-man's-land standing in place of Edwin Begg's familiar view. The legal problems of leases sold to and by at least nine separate companies means that while no further development has added to the Square's decline, attempts to redress the damage and activate the Council's preservation orders which they ignored, have failed through lack of funds. The project, begun in the name of freedom and civic high-mindedness, always a mark of the scoundrel, remains a symbol and a monument to the asset-stripped 80s. As yet only Frank Cornelius, Begg's close associate, has paid any satisfactory price for ruining so many lives.

'Barbican was born for that age.' Edwin Begg drew down the blind against his ruined prospect and sat on his bed, his frail body scarcely denting the great Belgian pillows at his back. 'Like a fly born to a dungheap. He could not help himself, my dear. It was his instinct to do what he did. Why are we always surprised by his kind?'

He had grown weak but eagerly asked if I would return the following Wednesday when he would tell me more about his visions and their effect upon his life. I promised to bring the ingredients. of a meal. I would cook lunch. He was touched and amused by this. He thought the idea great fun.

I told him to stay where he was. It was easy to let myself out.

'You know,' he called as I was leaving, 'there's a legend in our family. How we protect the Grail which will one day bring a reconciliation between God and Lucifer. I have no Grail to pass on to you but I think I have its secret.'

CHAPTER THREE

Astonishing Revelations of the Clapham Antichrist;
Claims Involvement in the Creation of a New
Messiah; His Visions of Paradise & Surrendering
His Soul for Knowledge; Further Description of the
Sporting Club Square Madonna; Final Days of the
Antichrist; His Appearance In Death

'Perhaps the crowning irony,' said the Clapham Antichrist of his unfrocking, 'was how devoted a Christian I was then! I argued that we shouldn't wait for God or heroes but seek our solutions at the domestic level. Naturally, it would mean empowering everyone, because only a thoroughly enfranchised democracy ever makes the best of its people. Oh, well, you know the sort of thing. The universal ideal that we all agree on and never seem to achieve. I merely suggested we take a hard look at the systems we used! They were quite evidently faulty! Not an especially revolutionary notion! But it met with considerable antagonism as you know. Politics seems to be a war of labels, one slapped on top of another until any glimmer of truth is thoroughly obscured. It's no wonder how quickly they lose all grip on reality!'

'And that's what you told them?'

He stood in his dressing gown staring down at a Square and gardens even BBIC had failed to conquer. The trees were full of the nests crows had built since the first farmers hedged the meadow. His study, with its books and big old-fashioned stereo, had hardly changed but had a deserted air now.

I had brought the ingredients of our lunch and stood in my street clothes with my bag expecting him to lead me to the kitchen, but he remained in his window and wanted me to stay. He pointed mysteriously towards the Duke's Elm and Gilbert's War Memorial, a fanciful drinking fountain that had never worked.

'That's what I told them, my dear. In the pulpit first. Then in the travelling shows. Then on the street. I was arrested for obstruction in 1937, refused to recognise the court and refused to pay the fine. This was my first brief prison sentence. Eventually I got myself in solitary.

'When I left prison I saw a London even more wretched than before. Beggars were everywhere. Vagrants were not in those days tolerated in the West End, but were still permitted in the doorways of Soho and Somers Town. The squalor was as bad as anything Mayhew reported. I thought my anger had been brought under control in prison but I was wrong. The obscene exploitation of the weak by the strong was everywhere displayed. I did whatever I could. I stood on a box at Speaker's Corner. I wrote and printed pamphlets. I sent letters and circulars to everyone, to the newspapers, to the BBC. Nobody took me very seriously. In the main I was ignored. When I was not ignored I was insulted. Eventually, holding a sign in Oxford Street, I was again arrested but this time there was a scuffle with the arresting policeman. I went into Wormwood Scrubs until the outbreak of the Blitz when I was released to volunteer for the ambulance service. Well, I wasn't prepared to return to prison after the War and in fact my ideas had gained a certain currency. Do you remember what Londoners were like then, my dear? After we learned how to look after ourselves rather better than our leaders could? Our morale was never higher. London's last war was a war the people won in spite of the authorities. But somewhere along the line we gave our achievements over to the politicians, the power addicts. The result is that we now live in rookeries and slum courts almost as miserable as our 19th century ancestors', or exist in blanketed luxury as divorced from common experience as a Russian Tsar. I'm not entirely sure about the quality of that progress, are you? These days the lowest common denominators are sought for as if they were principles.'

'You're still an example to us,' I said, thinking to console him.

He was grateful but shook his head, still looking down at the old elm as if he hoped to see someone there. 'I'll never be sure if I did any good. For a while, you know, I was quite a celebrity until they realised I wasn't offering an anti-Christian message and then they mostly lost interest. I couldn't get on with those Jesuits they all cultivated. But I spoke to the Fabians twice and met Wells, Shaw, Priestley and the rest. I was very cheerful. It appeared that I was spreading my message. I didn't understand that I was merely a vogue. I was quite a favourite with Bloomsbury and there was talk of putting me on Radio Luxembourg. But gradually doors were closed to me and I was rather humiliated on a couple of occasions. I hadn't started all this for fame or approval, so as soon as I realised what was happening I retired to the travelling shows and seaside fairgrounds which proliferated in England in the days before television.

'Eventually I began to doubt the value of my own pronouncements, since my audiences were dwindling and an evil force was progressing unchecked across Europe. We faced a future dominated by a few cruel dictatorships. Some kind of awful war was inevitable. During my final spell in clink I made up my mind to keep my thoughts to myself and consider better ways of getting them across. I saw nothing wrong with the message, but assumed myself to be a bad medium. In my free time I went out into the Square as much as I could. It was still easy to think there, even during the War.'

He took a step towards the window, almost as if he had seen someone he recognised and then he shrugged, turning his head away sharply and pretending to take an interest in one of his Sickerts. 'I found her there first, as you know, in 1933. And that one sight of her inspired a whole series of sermons. I came back week after week, but it always seemed as if I had just missed her. You could say I was in love with her. I wanted desperately for her to be real. Well, I had seen her again the evening I was "unfrocked". Of course I was in a pretty terrible state. I was praying. Since a boy I've always found it easy to pray in the Square. I identified God with the Duke's Elm – or at least I visualised God as a powerful old tree. I never understood why we placed such peculiar prohibitions on how we represented God. That's what they mean by "pagan". It has nothing to do with one's intellectual sophistication. I was praying when she appeared for the second time. First there was that strong scent of roses. When I looked up I saw her framed against the great trunk and it seemed a rose drew all her branches, leaves and blooms together and took human form!'

His face had a slight flush as he spoke. 'It seemed to me I'd been given a companion to help me make the best use of my life. She had that vibrancy, that uncommon beauty; she was a sentient flower.

'Various church examiners to whom I explained the vision understood my Rose either as an expression of my own unstable mind or as a manifestation of the devil. It was impossible for me to see her as either.

'She stepped forward and held out her hand to me. I had difficulty distinguishing her exact colours. They were many and subtle – an unbroken haze of pink and green and pale gold – all the shades of the rose. Her figure was slim but it wasn't easy to tell where her clothes met her body or even which was which. Her eyes changed in the light from deep emerald to violet. In spite of her extraordinary aura of power, her manner was almost hesitant. I think I was weeping as I went to her. I probably asked her what I should do. I know I decided to continue with my work. It was years before I saw her again, after I'd come out of prison for the last time.'

'But you did see her again?'

'Many times. Especially during the Blitz. But I'd learned my lesson. I kept all that to myself.'

'You were afraid of prison?'

'If you like. But I think it was probably more positive. God granted me a dream of the universe and her ever-expanding realities and I helped in the procreation of the new messiah!'

I waited for him to continue but he turned from the window with a broad smile. He was exhausted, tottering a little as he came with me to the kitchen and sat down in my place while I began to cook. He chatted amiably about the price of garlic and I prepared the dishes as he had taught me years before. This time, however, I was determined to encourage him to talk about himself.

He took a second glass of wine, his cheeks a little pinker than usual, his hair already beginning to rise about his head in a pure white fog.

'I suppose I needed her most during the War. There wasn't much time for talk, but I still came out to the Duke's Elm to pray. We began to meet frequently, always in the evenings before dark, and would walk together, comparing experience. She was from a quite different world — although her world sort of included ours. Eventually we became lovers.'

'Did she have a name?'

'I think so. I called her the Rose. I travelled with her. She took me to paradise, my dear, nowhere less! She showed me the whole of Creation! And so after a while my enthusiasm returned. Again, I wanted to share my vision but I had become far more cautious. I had a suspicion that I made a mistake the first time and almost lost my Rose as a result. When my nephew, who was in BBC Talks, offered me a new pulpit I was pretty much ready for it. This time I was determined to keep the reality to myself and just apply what I had experienced to ordinary, daily life. The public could not accept the intensity and implications of my pure vision. I cultivated an avuncularity which probably shocked those who knew me well. I became quite the jolly Englishman! I was offered speaking engagements in America. I was such a show-off. I spent less and less time in the Square and eventually months passed before I realised that I had lost contact with my Rose and our child! I felt such an utter fool, my dear. As soon as I understood what was happening I gave everything up. But it was too late.'

'You haven't seen her since?'

'Only in dreams.'

[93]

'What do you believe she was? The spirit of the tree?' I did my best to seem matter-of-fact, but he knew what I was up to and laughed, pouring himself more wine.

'She is her own spirit, my dear, make no mistake.'

And then the first course was ready, a *paté de foie gras* made by my friend Loris Murrail in Paris. Begg agreed that it was as good as his own. For our main course we had Quantock veal in saffron. He ate it with appreciative relish. He had not been able to cook much lately, he said, and his appetite was reduced, but he enjoyed every bite. I was touched by his enthusiasm and made a private decision to come regularly again. Cooking him lunch would be my way of giving him something back. My spirits rose at the prospect and it was only then that I realised how much I had missed his company.

'Perhaps,' he said, 'she was sent to me to sustain me only when I most needed her. I had thought it a mistake to try to share her with the world. I never spoke of her again after I had told the bishop about her and was accused of militant paganism, primitive nature-worship. I saw his point of view but I always worshipped God in all his manifestations. The bishop seemed to argue that paganism was indistinguishable from common experience and therefore could not be considered a religion at all!'

'You worshipped her?'

'In a sense, my dear. As a man worships his wife.'

I had made him a *tiesen sinamon* and he took his time with the meringue, lifting it up to his lips on the delicate silver fork which Begg's Cotswold benches had produced for Liberty in 1903. 'I don't know if it's better or worse, dear, but the world is changing profoundly you know. Our methods of making it safe just aren't really working any more. The danger of the simple answer is always with us and is inclined to lead to some sort of Final Solution. We are affected by turbulence as a leaf in the wind, but still we insist that the best way of dealing with the fact is to deny it or ignore it. And so we go on, hopelessly attempting to contain the thunder and the lightning and creating only further confusion! We're always caught by surprise! Yet it would require so little, surely, in the way of courage and imagination to find a way out, especially with today's wonderful computers?'

I had been depressed by the level and the outcome of the recent British election and was not optimistic. He agreed. 'How we love to cling to the wrecks which took us onto the rocks in the first place. In our panic we don't even see the empty lifeboats within easy swimming distance.'

He did not have the demeanour of a disappointed prophet. He remained lively and humorous. There was no sense of defeat about him, rather of quiet victory, of conquered pain. He did not at first seem disposed to tell me any more but when we were having coffee a casual remark set him off on a train of thought which led naturally back to that most significant event of his life. 'We aren't flawed,' he said, 'just as God isn't flawed. What we perceive as flaws are a reflection of our own failure to see the whole.' He spoke of a richly populated multiverse which was both within us and outside us. 'We're all reflections and echoes, one of another, and our originals, dear, are lost, probably forever. That was what I understood from my vision. I wrote it in my journal. Perhaps, very rarely, we're granted a glimpse of God's entire plan? Perhaps only when our need is desperate. I have no doubt that God sent me my Rose.'

I am still of a secular disposition. 'Or perhaps,' I suggested, 'as God you sent yourself a vision?'

He did not find this blasphemous but neither did he think it worth pursuing. 'It's much of muchness, that,' he said.

He was content in his beliefs. He had questioned them once but now he was convinced. 'God sent me a vision and I followed her. She was made flesh. A miracle. I went with her to where she lived, in the fields of colour, in the far Ether. We were married. We gave birth to a new human creature, neither male nor female but self-reproducing, a new messiah, and it set us free at last to dwell on that vast multiplicity of the heavens, to contemplate a quasi-infinity of versions of ourselves, our histories, our experience. That was what God granted me, my dear, when he sent me my Rose. Perhaps I was the antichrist, after all, or at least its parent.'

'In your vision did you see what became of the child?'

He spoke with lighthearted familiarity, not recalling some distant dream but describing an immediate reality. 'Oh, yes. It grew to lead the world upon a new stage in our evolution. I'm not sure you'd believe the details, my dear, or find them very palatable.'

I smiled at this, but for the first time in my life felt a hint of profound terror and I suppressed a sudden urge to shout at him, to tell him how ridiculous I considered his visions, a bizarre blend of popular prophecy and alchemical mumbo-jumbo which even a New Age traveller would take with a pinch of E. My anger overwhelmed me. Though I regained control of it he recognised it. He continued to speak but with growing reluctance and perhaps melancholy. 'I saw a peculiar inevitability to the process. What, after all, do most of us live for? Ourselves? And what use is that? What value? What profit?'

With a great sigh he put down his fork. 'That was delicious.' His satisfaction felt to me like an accolade.

'You're only describing human nature.' I took his plate.

'Is that what keeps us on a level with the amoeba, my dear, and makes us worth about as much individual affection? Come now! We allow ourselves to be ruled by every brutish, greedy instinct, not by what is significantly human in our nature! Our imagination is our greatest gift. It gives us our moral sensibility.' He looked away through the dining room window at the glittering domes of Gautier House and in the light the lines of his face were suddenly emphasised.

I had no wish ever to quarrel with him again. The previous argument, we were agreed, had cost us both too much. But I had to say what I thought. 'I was once told the moment I mentioned morality was the moment I'd crossed the line into lunacy,' I said. 'I suppose we must agree to understand things differently.'

For once he had forgotten his usual courtesy. I don't think he heard me. 'Wasn't all this damage avoidable?' he murmured. 'Weren't there ways in which cities could have grown up as we grew up, century adding to century, style to style, wisdom to wisdom? Isn't there something seriously wrong with the cycle we're in? Isn't there some way out?'

I made to reply but he shook his head, his hands on the table. 'I saw her again, you know, several times after the birth. How beautiful she was! How much beauty she showed me! It's like an amplification, my dear, of every sense! A discovery of new senses. An understanding that we don't need to discard anything as long as we continue to learn from it. It isn't frightening what she showed me. It's perfectly familiar once you begin to see. It's like looking at the quintessential versions of our ordinary realities. Trees, animals – they're there, in essence. You begin to discover all that. The fundamental geometry's identified. Well, you've seen this new maths, haven't you?'

He seemed so vulnerable at that moment that for once I wasn't frank. I was unconvinced by what I judged as hippy physics made possible only by the new creative powers of computers. I didn't offer him an argument.

'You can't help but hope that it's what death is like,' he said. 'You become an angel.'

He got up and returned slowly to his dusty study, beckoning me to look out with him into the twilight gathering around the trees where crows croaked their mutual reassurances through the darkening air. He glanced only once towards the old elm then turned his head away sharply. 'You'll think this unlikely, I know, but we first came together physically at midnight under a full moon as bright and thin and yellow as honesty in a dark blue sky. I looked at the moon through those strong black branches the moment before we touched. The joy of our union was indescribable. It was a confirmation of my faith. I made a mistake going back into public life. What good did it do for anyone, my dear?'

'We all made too many easy assumptions,' I said. 'It wasn't your fault.'

'I discovered sentimental solutions and comforted myself with them. Those comforts I turned to material profit. They became lies. And I lost her, my dear.' He made a small, anguished gesture. 'I'm still waiting for her to come back.'

He was scarcely aware of me. I felt I had intruded upon a private moment and suggested that I had tired him and should leave. Looking at me in surprise but without dispute he came towards me, remarking in particular on the saffron sauce. 'I can't tell you how much it meant to me, my dear, in every way.'

I promised to return the following Wednesday and cook. He licked his pink lips in comic anticipation and seemed genuinely delighted by the prospect. 'Yum, yum.' He embraced me suddenly with his frail body, his sweet face staring blindly into mine.

I had found his last revelations disturbing and my tendency was to dismiss them perhaps as an early sign of his senility. I even considered putting off my promised visit, but was already planning the next lunch when three days later I took a call from Mrs Arthur Begg who kept an eye on him and had my number. The Clapham Antichrist had died in his sleep. She had found him at noon with his head raised upon his massive pillows, the light from the open window falling on his face. She enthused over his wonderful expression in death.

In memorium, Horst Grimm

Edwin Begg was still very much alive when the next story was told, not by Sexton Begg himself (who later obliged me with certain details) but by an old man called 'Tozer' Vine, who had been a cabman employed by Sexton Begg in the old consulting detective days, before he was asked to take over from his brother at the Home Office.

In some of its details the story is not very different to many we heard during the age of European dictators, but it had its unusual aspects and involved a cousin of Begg's — a somewhat exotic figure who apparently turned up in more than one guise during Begg's career . . .

6. *the affair of the seven virgins*

Black it stood as night,
Fierce as ten Furies, terrible as hell,
And shook a dreadful dart; what seem'd his head
The likeness of a kingly crown had on.
Satan was now at hand, and from his seat
The monster moving onward, came as fast
With horrid strides; hell trembled as he strode.
                                    Milton,
                                Paradise Lost

CHAPTER ONE

A Queer Visitor

In all his long career as a private detective, Mr Sexton Begg had never received a stranger visitor to his Baker Street consulting rooms. Though it was not yet noon the personage now addressing him across the desk was clad in full evening suit, complete with cloak and silk hat. This alone was remarkable, but what was truly striking about the creature, who spoke with the faintest of educated Middle European accents, was that he was a pure albino!

From the visitor's bone-white skin stared eyes as crimson as the lining of his hat and cloak. Upon his long, delicate fingers he wore two rings, one of plain gold and the other in some black, mysterious metal, engraved with the crest of a family which had been old and civilised before the Romans ever attempted – and failed – to conquer

[99]

its land.

Sexton Begg felt himself in the presence of a great power – which could command the wealth of Europe, who smoked, after polite enquiry of his host, an oddly-smelling little brown cigarette which Begg, long familiar with Limehouse, recognised as opium. This doubtless explained the man's languor, his slightly hooded, if sardonically amused, eyes which regarded Begg with a certain understanding. The albino introduced himself, handing his card to the famous investigator.

The ivory pasteboard bore a simple inscription:

Monsieur Zenith,
The Albany

The hint of a smile crossed Begg's lips as he read the name. 'You prefer to be incognito, your highness?'

'You are discreet, Mr Begg. I can see that your reputation is not baseless.'

'I hope not, sir. By the way, as a fellow fiddle player, would I be right in thinking you are at present having trouble with your E-flat? A trifle sharp?'

The albino examined his little finger. 'Just so, Mr Begg.' He raised his right eyebrow a fraction. 'I am impressed.'

'No need to be, sir. An easily learned and very simple observation. The calluses on your hands are not, after all, dissimilar to my own! The rest was schoolboy logic. You are presumably here to seek my professional advice?'

'Exactly, sir.' Whereupon, 'Monsieur Zenith' dispensed with further formalities and launched, in precise, economical English, into his explanation for making this appointment. Sexton Begg's success was legendary. On more than one occasion he had been employed by the government of which M Zenith had until lately been a member. Blackshirt revolutionists had, with finance from a certain Great Power, succeeded in ousting the elected government and sending the king into exile. Now a puppet sat on the throne of Monsieur Zenith's mountainous land and a dictator, supported by foreign gold and arms, tyrannised a pleasant, if backward, nation, enslaving and destroying, creating dissension amongst people once living in easy harmony. Dr Papadakia had divided in order to rule. And rule he did

– in a land drowning in its own blood and shrieking in its death agonies.

This, said Monsieur Zenith, was what any intelligent reader could deduce from the newspapers. What was not generally understood was how, to make further capital from his country's suffering, the Dictator and his bullies were in essence kidnapping prominent people and ransoming them to relatives abroad. On more than one occasion tortured, ruined corpses had been delivered to those unable or unwilling to pay.

'That alone is an horrific trade, Mr Begg, I think you'll agree. There is a streak of ancient blood in our people which occasionally re-emerges. When it does, such cruelties become commonplace. What Papadakia and his gang are doing is offensive to all we civilised men hold holy.' The queer looking creature paused, lowering his eyes and drawing deeply on his little cigarette. After a while he continued. 'But now, Mr Begg, they have devised a variation on their vile theme.

'They are blackmailing the king!'

Their puppet – a distant cousin of the legitimate monarch – had rebelled and died. But having succeeded so well in their obscene enterprise, these bandits-in-uniform had sent a message to King Jhargon the Fourth (now with his family in Paris): 'Unless he returns to my country and gives his blessing to the present dictatorship, so that the world might think them reformed, Dr Papadakia and his bully-boys would, painfully and brutally, dispose of a young woman every day. Virgin blood, they declared, would be upon the king's hands.'

Long familiar with the world's infamies, Begg felt his own blood chill in his veins as Monsieur Zenith described the fate of the women, all members of his country's oldest families, who would die foully if he did not return. It was a scheme of almost unimaginable fiendishness and Begg's loathing for the 'fascisti' rabble informed the set of his lips and the hardening of his cool, grey eyes.

'You have my help in whatever form you desire, sir.' The detective's tone had grown singularly grave. 'Though I do not have the resources to start a counter-revolution in your country, if that is what you are proposing.'

'Those ideas are being debated elsewhere,' Monsieur Zenith told the detective. 'And moves are afoot to oust the dictator. But meanwhile there are seven young women, two of whom are directly related to me, who will die dreadfully if we do not help them. Dictator Papadakia already has the seven under lock and key. They are imprisoned in the Martyrs' Tower, from which in olden times the famous Ziniski monks jumped to their deaths rather than submit to the Injinkskya Heresy. Well, if you know that story you know that the tower is impregnable. Protected, they say, by Hell and History.' The albino casually extinguished the remains of his drugged cigarette in Begg's ashtray.

'You are telling me that the position of these young women is hopeless, Monsieur?' Begg's eyes narrowed.

'Unless the king capitulates.'

'Which he must not do – for the sake of his people and his honour.'

'Precisely, Mr Begg.'

Begg mused upon his caller's appalling position. 'Rescuing those seven maidens would be one thing,' he murmured. 'Ensuring that this foul dictator was ousted from his unearned eminence and foiled from committing any further evil – that would be another!'

Monsieur Zenith's expression did not change, but his posture appeared more relaxed and there was a certain amused alertness in his strange, crimson eyes. 'You are a man after my own heart, Mr Begg. I came to you for advice, as I said. What would you suggest?'

Begg placed his elbows on his desk. He put his fingertips together and regarded the albino over hands that seemed poised to pray. 'I have the glimmerings of an idea. But to explore it I must take a little time. And then, my dear sir, I shall require you to put me in your confidence on certain delicate matters. If convenient, I should be obliged if you could meet me again in twenty-four hours. Then we might discuss our plot . . .'

The albino rose, picked up his hat and bowed. 'I am obliged to you, Mr Begg. Until I came through your door I had no hope at all. Now I have a little.'

'Your opinion is flattering, sir. I sincerely hope I deserve it.' With a quick, almost clumsy movement, Begg reached to shake the albino's hand.

CHAPTER TWO

To Spin A Web

Less than four hours after his meeting with the albino, Sexton Begg would have been unrecognisable as the clean-cut gentleman who had interviewed Monsieur Zenith. Not that his appearance was inappropriate to his surroundings, which were slovenly, the foulest kind of thieves' den, and stank of a thick mixture combining opium, nicotine, alcohol and fried food. The vast maze of underground chambers, some of which connected directly with sewers and other routes which formed the secret roads of London's criminal intercourse, was known by the title of Smith's Kitchen. Smith himself, a seedy, corpulent individual who kept control of his premises by a mixture of blackmail and brute violence, was a kind of aristocrat. Although the police had sought to catch him over and over again, he had never been arrested. It was rumoured he had a hand in almost every kind of crime in London. He barred nobody from his place, so long, he said, as they kept their noses clean. Deadly rivals met at Smith's, but they had sense enough to keep their grudges to themselves.

Begg's reason for adopting the disguise of a petty sneak-thief and coming to Smith's was to meet a particular creature who went by the name of William Duck but was generally known as 'Dirty'. Duck was considered disgusting even by Smith's regulars, yet for some reason he was party to the kind of information about the 'upstairs' world of power, parliament and people in high places denied the most assiduous of modern journalists. Although suspected of it more than once, he was not an informer. But he knew the name of almost every prominent person staying on any particular night at any one of twenty London hotels.

Through the haze of smoke, Begg watched as a young girl got up from a table and made her weary way to the dance floor. Meanwhile Smith's band, an accordionist, a snare-drummer and a violinist, struck up another dusty tune and soon the crooks and their molls were in each others' arms, shuffling around the floor in a parody of pleasure.

In a doorway overhead a silhouette passed, then, stepping quickly down the rickety staircase crossed the room to where, in shadows, Begg waited.

From habit, Dirty Duck was incapable of anything resembling a direct route and approached Begg's table via the bar, where he bought himself a pint of beer, looking around as if for a seat. Only then did he make his way towards Begg.

All denizens of Smith's had a habit of talking softly from the corners of their mouths. The conversation between Begg and Duck took place in that style, using a whole variety of jargon and cant which, to an outsider, would have sounded like a foreign language. The exchange was brief. Money passed. And then, if anyone had been observing, Begg appeared to vanish. A moment later and Duck had vanished also.

Only one party had taken an interest in the conversation. His head moved to follow what had almost certainly been Duck's route out of the Kitchen. He wore smoked glasses and gave the impression that he was blind but, as his fingers flew over the accordion's keys in a lively Empire Medley, the eyes behind the glasses were deep in thought.

Half-an-hour later, Begg had reverted to his usual smart appearance, his favourite 'Petersen' stuck comfortably in the corner of his mouth, and lay deep in his Voysey armchair, a glass of single malt whisky readily to hand, poring over a large book. From time to time he would reach and consult his latest International Airways Guide. After a while he got up and put a gramophone record on his machine. Then, as the strains of Messiaen's *La Source du Vie* began to fill the room, he returned his attention to his books and documents.

When, that evening, his confidant and sometime assistant, the cabby Tozer Vine, knocked on the door of Begg's Sporting Club Square apartments he was shown in by Mrs Curry, Begg's housekeeper. Begg himself was fast asleep in his chair, his pipe unlit, his whisky scarcely tasted. But there was a large pad, full of notes, beside him now and an expression of satisfaction on his aquiline features.

Begg woke immediately, as if aware of Tozer's presence. 'Ah, the trusty Tozer! Did you get my message, old friend?'

'Yes, Mr Begg, and I did just as you asked. We might expect delivery between eight and nine tomorrow morning.'

'Excellent!' Begg was alert and fresh. He had long mastered the art of catching what sleep he could where he could, making the most of it. 'Now Tozer, I want you to take an envelope for me and deliver it to an address in Whitechapel which I shall give you. You must not linger there and if asked you will deny any knowledge of the one who gave you the envelope. Merely say that a customer paid you to deliver it.'

'Right you are, Mr Begg.' The cabby's massive face split in a grin.

His red cheeks positively glowed with pleasure. He loved nothing better than being party to Sexton Begg's cases.

When the amiably ugly cabby had departed on his errand, Begg frowned for a moment and glanced at his watch. Then he settled back into his chair and returned to the Land of Dreams.

CHAPTER THREE

A Fresh Twist

Monsieur Zenith arrived exactly on time. At Begg's suggestion he had come directly to the flat in Sporting Club Square.

Begg personally took charge of the albino's hat, cloak and ebony cane (noting its peculiar silver crest). Monsieur Zenith moved with his usual alertness, as if all senses were finely tuned, his strange eyes taking note of everything, yet remaining apparently languid. In Begg's sitting room he paused until the detective had indicated the easy chair opposite his own and then he went to sit down. His manner was graceful and insouciant, yet in no way offering discourtesy to his host. When Begg spoke, the albino listened intensely and with respect, nodding from time to time and interjecting the occasional word of enquiry or embellishment. What he heard appeared to impress and delight him.

'Excellent,' he murmured. 'Doubly excellent! Mr Begg, you are a gentleman after my own heart. It's a daring plan, but I think it will work.'

'We shall need to rehearse all this,' Begg added. 'And that is when your own intimacy with the king and his family will be crucial. Are you willing to discuss such matters and empower this individual with the necessary secrets?'

'Absolutely! I must admit my mind was running along similar lines. After all, if I am careful, the information will be of no special use to anyone. But what next? What shall we do?'

Begg waved his copy of the International Airways Guide. 'What we do, Monsieur, is take tomorrow's aerial packet. The journey will encompass three days, in all, because of the poor connections. That leaves us two more days before that fiend's deadline expires.'

'And what am I to do in the meantime, Mr Begg?'

'Contact the dictator's people. Tell them what we have agreed. And tell them the time and the date we shall be arriving in your capital. Do you have the necessary means, Monsieur, of achieving this within a few hours?'

'I have certain codes and access to a telegraph. If you will permit me, Mr Begg, I shall be on my way at once. I shall report to you here by suppertime – when I hope you will join me at a pleasant restaurant not a stone's throw from your door. Do you know it? The Tambourine? They serve the most delicious goulasch.'

'I should be delighted, sir.' Mr Begg closed his front door on his visitor. He frowned for a moment, then smiled to himself, nodding as he returned to his Voysey chair and his fire. 'Of course,' he murmured. 'Of course.'

Reaching for his smoking materials, he chuckled to himself. 'It seems this is to be an intriguing and stimulating affair, Monsieur.'

Monsieur Zenith was back somewhat later than planned. He had telephoned ahead and now entered Begg's door with a murmured apology for the lateness of the hour. There was a shadow in his eyes. It might have been concern or even hopelessness. As soon as he was seated he leaned forward, lit one of his little brown cigarettes, and proceeded to explain.

'I did exactly as I told you I would do, Mr Begg. I was lucky. Within an hour of leaving here I had telegraphed to a secret address on the continent and had received a reply. The dictator has agreed to our proposal but – as a "sign of good faith" – he has also demanded a hundred thousand pounds in Bank of England ingots! That is impossible for me to organise. My funds are frozen, my friends could not produce the necessary cash in time! Of course, in normal circumstances, I could arrange a draft on my Paris bank. In England, at present, I have no credit to speak of. Where could I, a hapless exile, borrow such a sum in gold?'

It was almost as if Begg had anticipated the problem. After a few minutes thought he picked up his telephone and spoke rapidly into the instrument. He listened carefully for a moment, uttered a brief word of assent and thanks, dashing a note on a pad in his elegant copperplate.

'If you take some form of identification to this address, your highness, I think you will find yourself very soon in possession of the necessary bullion. My brother Sir Warwick will expect you. The hour is late and we must be as fresh as possible for our adventure tomorrow. When you have received the bullion it will be your responsibility to oversee its transfer to the 8.30 airship from Victoria.'

The albino was clearly astonished by Sexton Begg's powers of persuasion – not to mention the value of his word of honour. 'Mr Begg, I cannot tell you the extent of my respect for your efficiency and the excellence of your connections. Needless to say my adopted country and myself shall be forever grateful to you. You are risking your reputation on behalf of a small nation of which half the world has never heard!'

'I risk nothing, sir. Because we shall succeed!' And with that Begg leapt from his chair and hastened to his bureau, there to write two notes – one to his amanuensis, Tozer Vine, the other to a high-ranking member of the British Government. The envelopes sealed and stamped, he disappeared into his private chamber to emerge wearing his Crombie and battered trilby. 'I can just catch the midnight collection. These will be in the right hands by morning!' He accompanied his guest out of the door to where a comfortable motor-cab waited, its engine softly running. At the wheel was the shrouded figure of Tozer Vine, his breath steaming in the cool spring air, his yellow lights cutting through a faint mist which clung to the trees of the square. Handing up one of the letters, Begg instructed his friend and chronicler to take Monsieur Zenith to the address shown on the envelope. The other he would put in the corner pillar box himself.

He watched as the cab started up and began to move off, Vine making expert play with the gear-lever. 'Good luck, Monsieur. I will see you at Victoria in the morning. We shall lunch in Paris!'

But Begg had first to call upon the services of that beneficial wonder-drug Koa-Kaine which, when used in moderation, had a powerful effect upon the intellect. Only in the hands of the addict-type could it become the very opposite of beneficial. Not for nothing was it known as the Devil's Snow. But Begg was a qualified doctor of medicine, specialising in the natural drugs of South and Central America, and had produced the definitive handbook upon the subject. As he carefully prepared his dosage, he attuned his powerful mind to a singular problem which, within a few hours, he hoped to solve by an effort of logic and imagination of which few were capable. These mental powers had made Begg's mind as admired internationally as his physical skill and daring. He had two or three ancient books to hand and a leather case containing a certain much sought-after scroll whose whereabouts were generally considered an insoluble mystery. One book bore only the picture of an ornate goblet stamped into its leather and no title, as such, within, merely a description of the book – which was a testimony written down by a Brother Olivier of

Renschel Abbey – the long confession of a certain Count Ulrich von Bek, made upon his death-bed in 1680. The others were of early and late 19th century appearance, all having in common the same crest, suggesting they came from a single library. Using his expertise at speed-reading, Begg settled to absorb the texts.

By two the next morning, as the oil in his lamp began to run out and he was forced to employ the gas, Begg had his theory. His eyes were still bright with the remains of the wonder-drug, though the effects were already fading. However, it was not the Devil's Snow which fuelled his elated emotions. It was the pure delight of an exceptional creature doing what it did best. As a fine greyhound pursues the hare, so did Sexton Begg pursue the truth!

CHAPTER FOUR

Conventional Treacheries

Sexton Begg settled back in his comfortable aerated chair and relished the passing view below. 'Another hour and we shall be in the French capital, Monsieur.' He addressed the albino who relaxed in the chair opposite. Monsieur Zenith wore a pair of plain, round smoked glasses to protect his eyes against the glaring sunlight pouring into the window. The albino had turned his head and was taking an interest in another passenger, who had boarded with them at the same time. Suddenly, he seemed unusually nervous. Perhaps the burden of his responsibility, having given his own note in return for a hundred thousand pounds-worth of English gold, was weighing upon him.

Begg leaned forward to catch Monsieur Zenith's attention. 'In precisely five hours, you and I shall have conferred with the king and his family. Then, in the company of a third individual, whom we shall meet at the station, we shall take the Orient Express to your country's capital. At this point we shall be met by the dictator's guards, forewarned of our company. The bullion will be transferred to a waiting van. We three will accompany it to its destination – the Kraskaya Fortress – where the exchange will be made. Your task, Monsieur, will be to get the gold out of the dictator's hands and into those of your counter-revolutionary council. Once the council is in power, you will control the treasury, so the British Government is sure of her investment in your courage and integrity, Monsieur.'

'I'm honoured, Mr Begg.' The albino waved a languid cigarette. Once again, he seemed to have lost all sense of urgency, and took only the most casual interest in the fate of his kinswomen. Perhaps the opium was his means of 'switching off' his brain, just as Begg used the mantras and prayer-balls of the High Kandooni, the so-called Abominable Snowmen who inhabited the upper reaches of the Himalayas. 'You can rely upon me, I think. Your task, Mr Begg, will be to ensure the safety of the young women. That, we have agreed, is of top priority. Once I know they are on their way to freedom, I can complete my own job at the fortress. It will be some little while, I fear, before I can join you. I must stay with our third party as long as possible, or our plan will not work and his life will be forfeit.'

After this perfectly coherent speech, Monsieur Zenith turned his bespectacled eyes upon the heavens and appeared to stare lazily at the elemental vision which, until a few years earlier, had been the prerogative of birds, of angels and of the Almighty.

A little while later, Begg saw the spires and elegant towers of the City of Light glittering upon the horizon and he felt the elation of all travellers when they recall the beauty and civilised taste of Europe's most gorgeous modern capital.

'Paris next stop. Next stop Paris, sir,' cried the smartly-uniformed steward as he proceeded along the aisle. 'Don't forget your hat, sir. Don't forget your bag. Paris, ladies and gentlemen. Next stop Paris. Remember to take your property. Paris. Paris next stop.'

The sun caught the crystalline facets of the towers. As the airship manoeuvred towards the mast at Orly field, Paris appeared to burn with all the colours of the spectrum, like a single, mighty gem.

Sexton Begg glanced at his watch. 'Bang on time,' he said. 'We shan't miss our lunch, after all.'

Their business in Paris concluded, Sexton Begg and Monsieur Zenith now shared a private compartment with a third man, clad in a grey, military greatcoat and a badgeless grey, military hat, his face shaded by both lapels and peak. He rarely spoke, when they were before any other person, but seemed disconsolate, ill-at-ease. The guard who took their tickets believed that Begg and the albino were high-ranking officials escorting a disgraced prisoner back to his country, but he had detected no sign of manacles. Doubtless the military gentleman was on his honour.

The Orient Express provided the most comfortable and delicious means of travelling to what seemed almost certain death, but Begg and Zenith were both in good spirits and, when alone with the other man, shared a private, rather black joke or two.

As already recorded, Begg's spirits always rose when in pursuit of the truth. But Monsieur Zenith was fired by a different prospect. While he clearly cared for the liberation of his adopted country and the release of his blood-relatives, there was another matter on his mind – one he had not shared with the famous detective.

The box, carried as cargo by airship, was now at their feet. It was oblong and wrapped in scarlet velvet, bound with ropes of gold and silver. In the lid was emblazoned a single motif, the crest of a certain noble European family to which both Begg and Monsieur Zenith belonged. Their papers described an heirloom being returned to its original home. Yet it was not the bullion which interested the albino. Indeed, the man in the greatcoat (who perhaps did not know what the box contained) showed more curiosity towards it than either of his companions.

The Orient Express pulled into the station at dusk when the capital was already beginning to shut down under the vicious curfew of the new regime. The city had never recovered from the civil war which had shaken it in the early part of the century. Once she had boasted the flower of European architecture from Gothick to the *Belle Époque*, but now only her ruins were picturesque and the new city was a monotony of red brick and stark concrete modelled upon the German modernist schools.

Descending to the platform, Begg, Monsieur Zenith and their mysterious companion watched as porters loaded the box upon a sturdy hand-cart and began to push it along the pitted marble towards the exit.

As the trio gave up their tickets to the attendant, a loud cry rang out, echoed in the high ceilings of a more elegant age. And a sudden silence fell upon the whole station.

Then, through the passenger arch of the main gate, there appeared a great, gleaming Rolls Royce. The open tourer, of the kind once used by staff commanders in the Great War, was painted a gaudy yellow and black – the colours of the fascisti warlords who had seized power from the democratically elected government. Banners fluttered all over the car. It was surrounded by an escort of motor-cycle riders with the forked cross of their ruling Party on their armbands and helmets. Behind them, similarly uniformed, rode a crack cavalry regiment which had been 'loaned' by a foreign power friendly to the regime and had a reputation of utter ruthlessness when 'crowd discipline' was the issue. Their hardened, scarred faces glared from helmets as brightly polished as the steel tips of their lances. Before this swaggering entourage the public melted, hurrying in all directions, taking any exit rather than arouse the passing irritation of just one of those riders, who had carte-blanche to perform any infamy they pleased.

The Rolls Royce drove up to within an inch of where Begg, Monsieur Zenith and their companion waited. No-one flinched.

The fierce, arrogant stare of the car's main occupant was met and returned as a fearless challenge. He was not used to such resistance and found an excuse to address one of his aides who saluted and spoke to the trio.

'We are glad you have decided to do your patriotic duty, gentlemen.' The dictator's aide spoke with a distinct Bavarian accent. 'And we are pleased to welcome you to the new, invigorated nation where we are sweeping away all the old symbols and systems and heralding in new, modern ideas which will soon make us one of the richest and most dynamic countries in Europe.'

'I should hardly think you would require the services of a king, gentlemen.' The voice was amused, a little brutal, a little defiant. The speaker folded down his lapels, pushed back his cap, took a slow pull on his cigarette holder and smiled directly at the aide. But it was the dictator who gasped with triumph.

'Good evening, your majesty,' he said.

CHAPTER FIVE

Reversals and Revelations

The Martyrs' Tower was as grim as its name, a massive pile of unclad granite, pierced by a few slender windows until the top, where a narrow, castellated walkway allowed prisoners a minimum of exercise. It was from here that the famous martyrs had jumped to their deaths rather than renounce their innocent and reverential belief in the Injinkskya Heresy, which had since become incorporated into the orthodoxy of the church.

Now containing Dictator Doktor Johen Papadakia, a small, stooped individual with trembling, claw-like hands who led the local

Master Race, with his aide, a certain Fritz von Papen, the Rolls Royce drove the three arrivals through cold, rainy streets where normal illuminations were abolished and roving search lights moved between the bleak, characterless brick blocks, where soldiers killed on sight anyone not in the uniform of the fascisti.

'You are a man of your word, I know, Mr Begg,' said Dictator Papadakia, combing at his straggling grey beard and casting a cunning glance at the box now carried in the tourer's boot. 'And, I, of course, am the same. The little girls will be released the moment we have opened the box and noted the contents. We have our king home again and his re-instatement will be a costly business, as you can imagine. Here we are. The young ladies have been perfectly comfortable. They are so far unharmed – though they are very pretty and one or two of them have caught the eye of my lusty uhlans – they know how to handle a woman, eh?'

Later Sexton Begg would remark that he had never in his life expected to see an albino pale – but he swore that Zenith's bone-white features drained of any vestige of colour at this last remark. Yet still the nobleman controlled himself, while the king stared around at his old capital, apparently with a new-born interest, as if he had failed to take in the enormity of Papadakia's implied threat.

The grim-faced praetorians dismounted and formed a foot escort. The dictator and his aide led the party through the lowering portcullis of that pitiless pile until they crossed a small bailey, cobbled and dark red with the blood of centuries, to enter the daunting hallway of the tower, its roof low and dank, as if never built for Man.

Bats and other flying creatures flapped about in the mephitic eaves while upon the slimy flagstones things hopped and skittered and crawled.

'I must admit,' declared the dictator by way of apology, 'that not all of our tower is this salubrious. We keep this to show our visiting foreign guests. Sadly, the rest of the place is in somewhat poorer condition.' He led the way along a passage and up a circular staircase which wound forever, it seemed, above an unrailed drop whose bottom lay far below the tower's foundations. Behind them followed the guards, carrying the precious box. 'They say it's haunted.'

It was eminently clear that no-one could escape the Martyrs' Tower by this, the only means of coming and going. It was always guarded. Every few yards they passed uniformed soldiers armed with the very latest repeating rifles from a famous continental manufacturer. Their orders were the same as the curfew's – unless accompanied by men in the fascisti uniform, all who moved were to be shot on sight.

[112]

The king, noting this, murmured something to Begg who did his best to reassure the man. It was clear the king was beginning to regret his decision. Perhaps he had never seen the infamous haunted tower of Mirenburg at first hand before. After hearing him out, Begg spoke a few words which only the king caught. 'Courage! You cannot weaken now or all is lost. A few more hours and our plan will be successful – as long as we keep our nerve.'

His words appeared to strengthen the king's resolve. And now they were at the top of the tower, entering a circular room at the centre of which was a huge cage and within the cage, clad only in flimsy night-clothes, trembling miserably in the icy wind, were seven beautiful young women, like angels come to earth and caught in some supernatural fowler's net.

'You fiend!' The words burst from Monsieur Zenith's lips as his eyes fell upon that dastardly scene. His instinct was to whip off his cloak and pass it through the bars to the women. Next, his jacket went to comfort them.

Dictator Papadakia watched in contemptuous amusement as the men lent their outer garments to the seven virgins trembling against that cold steel.

'Soon they'll be back in their own little beds and proud to have served their country as they have. They are, after all, only *potential* martyrs.'

Zenith turned on his heel. The white of his shirt and waistcoat was now relieved only by his perfectly pressed trousers and his gleaming pumps. Although lean, he was perfectly muscled, showing that he took care of his body with a rigorous application of diet and exercise.

'You have everything you demanded of us, Monsieur Papadakia. Now I would ask of you the courtesy of a key.' And he held his pale hand to his foulest enemy.

Laughing crazily, Doktor Papadakia dropped the ring into Zenith's hand. 'A cheap price to pay, you must think, your highness – for *your daughter's safe release!*'

Only then did Begg note, by the slightest flicker of a muscle, the albino's jaw clench, and relax. Monsieur Zenith fitted another cigarette to his holder. The aide lit it for him, bringing the flame of the lighter hard against his bone-white skin. Still Monsieur Zenith did not flinch, did not for a moment betray that he felt the flame. After a while Fritz von Papen fell back like a defeated lover and with an animal snarl returned the lighter to his pocket.

Monsieur Zenith handed the key to Begg, who went to unlock the cage, glancing briefly at the box which had yet to be opened. As the door swung back and before the girls could fling themselves through, Dictator Papadakia cried 'Stop!' and again the world froze for a moment – save for Zenith the Albino, who continued to smoke his cigarette and watch the action as if he lazed in a box at the Opera and suffered an indifferent performance of Wagner.

'First, you will give me *your* key, your highness,' rasped the dictator, his bird-like hands clutching towards the albino. There was a rapid movement and, as if from nowhere, the small gold key had landed in the dictator's hands. He passed it to his aide, who knelt before the box, frowning over the insignia and making as if to cross himself, until he caught the dictator's secular eye.

The key turned easily and the lid was opened with little effort – to reveal ingot upon ingot of gleaming gold! English gold, from the greatest bank in the world. Dictator Papadakia's eyes glittered. He drooled with delight, considering the power such gold would bring him. He sniggered in triumph at his ability to coax so much wealth from the lair of the British lion, and to show his power over what he perceived as a government enfeebled by the lies of liberalism. Papadakia's simple love of gold was as banal as the rest of his miserable impulses, his spurious dreams, and Begg could not disguise the expression of contempt which spread across his features. It was quite obvious what the dictator's ambitions were. Other little, pompous fools like Mussolini had taken control of more than one nation, so why shouldn't he? With free weapons and this gold, he looked upon his neighbours with gleeful anticipation.

Begg stepped forward but was halted in his tracks by Zenith. 'No, Begg. Your job is to look after the women.'

Reluctantly Sexton Begg fell back, helping the young women out of the cage and across the stinking fester of the floor.

This was as far as the plan went, as far as they had agreed, but Begg had other intentions. As soon as they were past the guards and out beside the waiting Daimler, bearing the official crest of the country, he spoke a few brief words to the grateful virgins and ushered them into the car. But Begg did not drive off with them. Instead, he turned and marched back into the tower, for all the world as if he had official permission!

Begg shared few of his secrets. His only real confidant was Tozer Vine, the cab-driver who was also, perhaps, his closest friend. He would speak of the next incidents only to Vine and then after some days had passed. Often, he told Vine, he wished that he had left things as they were, escorted the women out of Mirenburg and had done with it. But his curiosity must be satisfied.

The plan he had not discussed with anyone, save the authorities in London, was now put into process. He made his way secretly back to the top of the tower where four men stood around an open box of bullion. Now none of them was in conflict, it seemed, but were sharing a comradely joke.

Begg's suspicions were confirmed. This kidnap plot was all a fiction dreamed up by the four who gloated over a hundred thousand golden pounds.

'You have done well, your highness,' congratulated the dictator. 'And you see I kept the bargain. That fool Begg has taken your daughter to safety, we have the English government's gold, and you can return into exile. Where will you go? As soon as Begg understands the truth, he will make sure it appears in the papers. Your reputation will be ruined.'

'My reputation was never perfect.' The albino spoke casually, taking a long pull on his holder. 'And twenty-five thousand in gold will be some small compensation. I hope I can be of service to you again very soon, monsieur.'

'I am sure we shall have further business in common, Monsieur Zenith. And I will be as good as my word. I will introduce you to my own "guardian angels", the Brotherhood of the Beast. They will be glad to adopt you into our ranks.'

'Well and good, gents.' The king now spoke in the louche accents of suburban Kent, 'but I've done my bit I think, playing the king as long as I have. Can old Captain Quelch have his little percentage and be on his way? I am planning to catch the next train back to civilisation.'

Whereupon Begg, hiding in an alcove behind a rotting hanging, saw a large packet of American dollars change hands. The 'king' was none other than Quelch the famous White Pirate, more lately a successful confidence trickster operating chiefly in the European 'midi', whom Begg had known to be King Jhargon's double. It was Begg, via Dirty Duck and Tozer Vine, who had located Quelch and commissioned him. But Monsieur Zenith had anticipated this part of the plan. Observing Begg in Smith's Kitchen, Zenith confirmed that Captain Quelch would be involved. Only then had he contacted Quelch and put the plan to him – to steal a hundred thousand pounds from the Bank of England. By using the reputation and honour of Sexton Begg!

Begg was unmoved. Almost all of this he had already determined. But now it was important that somehow he reach the bullion box. For there was one other item carried into the country which only

Begg (and his Whitechapel carpenter) knew about.

There was nothing for it but bluff.

Coolly Begg stepped into the room, confronting the four conspirators.

CHAPTER SIX

Manifestations and Mysteries

Monsieur Zenith was the first to respond to Begg's sudden reappearance. He smiled and bowed gracefully. 'Well, well, Mr Begg. You were, as always, thoroughly underestimated. But now that the truth of our little deception is out, what do you intend to do about it? I would emphasise that there is no escape from the Martyrs' Tower and you are rather considerably outnumbered. What of the girls?'

'I took the liberty of inviting my assistant, Tozer Vine, to follow in a special carriage with our Daimler. He is even now carrying the beautiful hostages across the border into friendly territory.'

'I am grateful to you, Mr Begg.'

'Enough of this ridiculous charade!' cried Fritz von Papen. 'What can you gain from this, Begg? You are doomed! You have returned only to die!' And he reached towards his holster, unbuttoning the flap. But the dictator's eyes were narrowing and he stopped his aide.

'No! He must have some other helping him. Perhaps there are spies amongst our people – or you, so-called Zenith the Turncoat. You turned once – you can turn again, eh?'

'If you'll finish this discussion without me, gentlemen, I'll be off.' With a tip of his military cap the king's double, Quelch, made his exit.

'That's improved the odds a little.' Begg permitted himself a small smile. 'Presumably you gentlemen have not looked closely at the bullion box just yet – or you will have noticed that those "ingots" are a masterpiece of the forger's art. I took the precaution of doing a little background research on your histories. I was not going to guarantee a hundred thousand pounds of our sovereign wealth without so doing. What I read and what I learned elsewhere led me to believe that there are dark forces at work across Europe. You, gentlemen, are at the very heart of the evil. If you will permit me—' With this, Begg stooped, released a secret catch which sprang open to drop into his hands a magnificent double barrelled hunting gun in gleaming steel, ivory and walnut. This he levelled at the dictator's chest.

'This is a Purdy's, Herr Papadakia, and as I'm sure you know there is no more reliable gun made. It is loaded with a particularly large shell of peculiar manufacture. It is capable of destroying an elephant, but is perhaps rather more suitable for hunting devils – if you follow me!'

Fritz von Papen fell back, ghastly pale, staring at the remaining conspirators. He took Begg's meaning completely and only now, it seemed, realised the nature of the creatures with whom he had been dealing.

Begg crisply ordered the aide to go – 'and take your uhlans with you when you do!'

Von Papen was quick to obey, scrambling down the steps and yelling for his men to follow. A moment later departing hooves clattered on cobbles.

An unearthly silence had fallen upon the tower. Still a small smile played about Begg's firm lips and it was mirrored in Zenith's own expression. The two men knew they were equally matched and had nothing but admiration one for the other.

'Angel shot,' said Dictator Papadakia with a shrug. 'Is that what you think? I'm some agent of Satan?'

'I believe you to be an agent of evil, certainly,' said Begg. 'And I also believe Monsieur Zenith here would have nothing to do with you, save that you kidnapped his daughter. Yet you are two of a kind, are you not?'

Now Monsieur Zenith was laughing openly. 'I believe only Captain Quelch will come out of this particular adventure with any profit. And I, of course, have my daughter safe. For that, Mr Begg, I owe you much. But you are mistaken if you think the equation demands three such supernatural forces. Quelch was the second for whom your other barrel was designed. I am the first. This creature – this horrible thing – is nothing. I had meant to perform my task alone. I fear it must be witnessed by the man I admire above all others on this planet. Yes, Mr Begg, you have the power to slay me. Only you have the knowledge and the resources to do that. It is true that one cartridge from your barrel will end my span of near-immortality. So I will allow you therefore to be both witness and judge of my revenge. For revenge it will be, Mr Begg, and a terrible one. Upon a creature who thought he could turn my family away from its work, from its massive burden of supernatural responsibility. Aha! I see that you understand, cousin. At least if I die, it will be with your respect, I think.'

To this last statement Begg assented by declining his head a fraction.

Whereupon he was flung back suddenly by a blinding force which drove him against the wall and almost tore the elephant gun from his hands and, if the safety had not been on, would have made him blow both deadly barrels.

The dictator was scampering for the exit but was drawn back, it seemed, by a long, silvery arm which flung him into the cage just recently vacated. Doktor Papadakia cowered at the bottom like a terrified canary while Zenith the Albino strolled towards him, grinning. The count's skin rippled with a thousand colours. His eyes glowed, shifting, distorted, faceted, as if they looked upon a million worlds at once. From the monster's shoulders spread two mighty wings, silver feathers clashing. At his belt was a blade, an ebony broadsword of massive proportions on which crimson runes, in some prehistoric language, writhed and seemed to murmur.

And Sexton Begg knew that he looked upon an Angel of Destruction – a creature of almost limitless power who might, centuries before, have been human, but had lived too long in the wilder reaches of the multiverse. Now Monsieur Zenith was a player in the Game of Time. The scroll had revealed much to Begg. It was a tale of a family doomed forever to do the Devil's work, seek nothing less than resolution and reconciliation between God and Satan.

As Begg watched, the creature's ruby eyes flared with terrible energy. The silver teeth clashed in a silver skull. A noise came from the silver throat.

It was neither human nor bestial, but the growling anger of an angel, of a jugador, a mukhamir, a seasoned player in the long Game of Time, where Law and Chaos warred across the multiverse.

And now the sword was lifted, almost ritualistically, howling and shrieking and singing in a key so alien, a melody so exquisite, that Begg almost allowed himself to drop the gun and cover his ears. Yet he weathered this storm of supernatural symphony and witnessed the creature that had been born His Highness Count Ulrich Rudric Renark Otto von Bek-Krasny, elected Protector of Wäldenstein, hereditary Prince of Mirenburg, Defender of the Grail, Blood-guard of the Holy Roman Emperor, King of Crete and Damascus, Order of the Moravian Hierarchy, Antagonist-in-Waiting to Pope Clement the Dane, Curator of the Ariochan Temple, Knight of Saint Odhran and Saint Mungo, President of his adopted State and master thief extraordinary, transform itself entirely into a creature of purely mythical proportions and appearance, slipping a mighty black sword into the cringing body of the dictator and drawing the filthy soul-stuff – not for itself, but to dispose of it as another might dispose of a fouled rag, flicking it into the farther ether.

The sword seemed to grumble as it feasted, as if it felt it deserved better nourishment, but it continued to drink, continued to discard, as the silver angel howled like the Wolf of All-Time and bayed out a song of revenge which was payment for the cruel horrors and infamies committed by the dictator and his minions. The sound was caught by every bell in the city, until they rang in crazy unison. And still the runesword drank. And still the albino howled.

When all the filth was gone, nothing much remained of the dictator Papadakia who had only lately pranced and raved and boasted and handed out casual death to all – now he was a limp, blank thing, passive and obedient. There was a wound in him.

He was allowed to slump into a chair. His eyes were fixed on a spot above Zenith's glowing head and when Begg followed the dictator's gaze he thought he saw, for an instant, the outline of a pulsing cup, covered in rubies and bearing a cross of silver and gold. When the vision was gone, Begg looked back. There was now no sign of a wound on Papadakia's body.

Begg could stand no more. He lowered the gun and turned to go. He did not know if Zenith were devil or angel or another kind of creature altogether. He only knew that he had never wanted the privilege of such a vision and would regret it for the rest of his life. Here was a truth which even the great Sexton Begg was reluctant to face. The 'gold' was worthless, a mere decoy to hide the gun. He could leave it. He wanted no more of the affair.

Then, to Begg's frank terror, the thing that was Papadakia lurched from its chair, hands grasping horribly at the air, eyes widening and rolling – its mouth the red maw of a rabid hyaena.

But it was not Begg it attacked – for suddenly the claws were turned upon its own throat. Begg watched in fascinated impotence as the dictator strangled himself relentlessly to death!

Looking up at last from the remains on the floor Begg found himself staring into the faintly amused eyes of Zenith the albino, a small brown cigarette gracing his elegant jade holder as he bowed and raised his silk hat a fraction. 'I think our work is completed here, don't you, Mr Begg? Already my government in exile returns. What you witnessed seemed the simplest way of settling the affair. To my regret your intellect is so finely tuned that you detected something of my intention. You made only one mistake, Mr Begg. You assumed that poor wretch to be one of us. I assure you – he is no player in the Game of Time. Merely a mortal who exploits our Game. But he is gone now. At this moment throughout the Kingdom our people are taking over. All's well that ends well, I think, Mr Begg. No hard feelings?'

Begg was removing the cartridges from his gun and slipping them into the pocket of his Norfolk. 'I am not altogether sure of that, Monsieur. You did hope, did you not, to defraud the British government of a large sum? Your associate Quelch is already on his way to freedom with his bit of blood-money, what? I will grant that you have put an end to an injustice but I cannot approve of your methods. I discovered your family's motto – *Opus Sathanus*. I had not expected to see it demonstrated so dramatically.'

And at that he reached out impulsively and took the strange albino's hand.

'We'll meet again, Monsieur Zenith, though I fear next time we shall not be on the same side.'

'Well, Mr Detective, let us hope we remain friends, even as we play the parts of enemies. Farewell, Sexton Begg. I will never forget the help you gave our family.'

Begg shrugged. It would be some years before he would be able fully to accept the fact that, here at the Martyrs' Tower he had for a few seconds set eyes upon the Holy Grail. Or that the Grail had been summoned by one whom the world knew as a criminal or worse.

He put the empty gun over his shoulder. He allowed a small smile to form on his manly lips.

'You forget, Monsieur,' he said gently, 'that it is my family also.'

Epilogue

It was not until they were back in Sporting Club Square and a discreet, if only partial, report lodged with the Foreign Office, that Sexton Begg told the whole story to Tozer Vine. The loyal cabby sat in his familiar Voysey on the other side of a glowing fireplace, enjoying a brandy and soda served by his old friend and hero.

'Well, sir, for all that,' mused Tozer, making a few deft notes in his personal shorthand, using the slender silver pencil and notebook presented to him by a very senior member of the Royal Family, 'that there count didn't seem a bad sort of cove, did 'e, guv'nor? After all, the dictator bloke *forced* Count Zenith to act. 'Is plan suited *'is* sense of honour but didn't endanger *your* life. 'E pitted 'imself against the best, didn't 'e! But 'e always made sure that nobody got 'urt – just the true villain – that Papadakia feller. What we in the trade call "the original instigator" of the evil. I don't fink the count's a rotten'un, guv'nor. But I fink 'e's learned to put 'isself an' his nearest an' dearest first in this crool world.' He winked. 'A true fallen angel, yer might say. Cynicism's 'is name, an' that's the shame of it. What a waste!'

'You'd have to admit, Tozer old man, that it's a rum sort of business all in all, what? Pretty unusual, even in our line of work?' Sexton Begg drew massive brows to the centre of that noble, intellectual forehead.

'Rummer than most, sir,' agreed Tozer. And, closing his eyes, the cabby displayed his amazing literary memory by quoting from Milton –

> 'Black it stood as night,
> Fierce as ten Furies, terrible as hell . . .'

Begg sat back in his chair, his whole attention upon the poem, his eyes shut, staring at impossible memories, even as he enjoyed the warmth of his familiar hearth, knowing how it was just possible that, for a few hours, he had entertained in his simple Hammersmith bachelor chambers, the Prince of the Morning personified. For the moment, an evil had been confounded and Chaos held at bay. One day, however, he and his noble albino adversary must inevitably fight to the finish. When Tozer was done, Sexton Begg's own, deep tones filled the darkening room. Firelight brought fierce resolution to his features and flung his massive purple shadow upon the Persianate walls as he, too, quoted from the great Christian epic, *Paradise Lost* . . .

> Impendent horrors! threatening hideous fall
> One day upon our heads; while we, perhaps,
> Designing or exhorting glorious war,
> Caught in a fiery tempest, shall be hurl'd
> Each on his rock transfix'd, the sport and prey
> Of racking whirlwinds; or for ever sunk
> Under yon boiling ocean, wrapt in chains,
> There to converse with everlasting groans.

[121]

He reached for his pipe, offering Tozer his pouch of Meng & Ecker's Special 'O'.

Soon the pleasant fumes of opium tobacco filled the study and the two men contemplated in profound silence the import of all that had befallen Sexton Begg at the Martyrs' Tower in Mirenburg, in the land of Wäldenstein, in the year of Our Lord 1937.

(With grateful acknowledgements to Anthony Skene)

'You may ask,' said Sexton Begg, 'what became of the seven virgins. Well, all of them emigrated to England before the War and all but one married English noblemen, settling into a life of somewhat stifling certainty for which they remained grateful all their lives. The seventh, I fear, had come too close to evil and had savoured the taste of it. She became an exotic dancer. The only use she had ever made of an oustanding education was to take for herself the name of Wheldrake's heroine from the famous late poem. You'll recall the lines —

> Sylvia Blade, Sylvia Blade,
> My own immortal soul I'd trade,
> For a single day with Sylvia Blade.

'Though Wheldrake, with his Northumbrian roots, took the name from an earlier ballad —

> Ladye Sylvia Bladde followed the darke
>   And bore on her breastte the Deville's mark.
> Her love was greatte for Lord John Becke,
>   Who dragged her alive from the Cawdrae Wrecke,
> And tooke her to wyffe and tooke her to warde
>   Under the power of his bra' blacke sworde,
> So dooming his soulle to its foulle rewarde.
>   Now he rides on the winde through Herninsglade,
>   Forever in thralle to Sylvia Bladde,
>   Still crying the name of Sylvia Bladde.

'She adopted her stage name as her own, went to America and eventually wound up working in a high-class strip-joint. That wasn't the worst that happened to her, though there are several versions of her story. Possibly the strangest version concerns a cousin of mine, Henry Beck, a reporter on the *Chicago Tribune* some years ago. The story is based on fact, but has appeared in several guises. I first received it in the post – an envelope containing a few sheets of foolscap on which had been written in old-fashioned copperplate the fundamentals of the tale. A note attached to the manuscript said that the author had published the story much earlier in, as he recollected, *Spicy Reporter* or possibly *Terror Detective*, one of the many American pulps he had contributed to during his stay in the USA. He had later re-sold it as a 'Hank Beck' story to the short-lived British magazine *Devil Dame Detective* (US title *Double Dime Detective*) which had published three issues during 1947. He had sold the story again to a men's magazine called *Thrust* in 1966 and was currently rewriting it as a cyberpunk story for *Isaac Asimov's Magazine*. Its original *Spicy* title had been . . .'

7. *the girl who killed sylvia blade*

CHAPTER ONE

She came through the door with a gun in her hand and tears in her eyes. I didn't know what I was going to get first – the gun or the tears. Thought of either depressed me.

I said: 'Hello, there . . .'

She was five feet tall in a green paisley trouser suit, with long blonde hair and a pastel pink skin. Her eyes were big and blue. Somehow she reminded me of Alice in Wonderland after a particularly hairy ordeal with the Queen of Hearts.

She didn't say anything. But she lowered the gun and began to cry.

I sighed and moved in, easing the little .38 from her soft hand. I put the tips of my fingers on her arm and guided her across the carpet to the big guest chair. She sat down with a bump. I went to the bar and poured her a large gin. I put it in the hand that had held the gun; it seemed a fair trade. She drank the gin, downing half of it in one swallow, and when she looked up at me she wasn't crying any more.

'You're Beck?' she said. 'The reporter on the *Trib*?' She had a whispering New England accent that did something to me. I nodded.

'I'm Belinda Fayre.'

'Uh-huh,' I said. 'I saw you at The Black Room two nights ago. I like the way you frug. What's your problem? Why come in without knocking? Why the gun?'

'I just killed someone.' She said it flatly, with a hint of surprise in those wide, blue eyes. 'At The Black Room. I shot her.'

I picked up the gun and sniffed it. 'Someone certainly fired this recently. Shot who?'

'Sylvia.'

'Wow,' I said. 'Sylvia Blade.' Sylvia Blade was a top star at the discotheque – The Black Room – where, to powerful beat music, Belinda frugged twice nightly in a golden cage above the dance floor. Sylvia's act was the most popular. It involved a long bull whip and a male partner. I'd only heard about it. That stuff isn't for me.

'I didn't mean to,' she said.

'They never do. You want help from me?'

'Yes.' The word was the sound of a summer breeze through a Maine meadow. She looked at the rug. 'I'm sorry – I –'

'Baby,' I said, 'so am I. You're not the first, you know. You killed a woman. You think I can get you off a rap like that? You think I would? I work with the law, honey, not against it.'

'But – I didn't mean to kill her. She attacked me. She – she was – she was vile, Mr Beck. The gun was hers – she kept it in her dressing room. She—'

'Why did she attack you?'

Belinda wasn't listening to me. She just kept talking, getting it out fast. Belinda had been dating a youngster who attended the disco; dating customers was against the rules. Sylvia had found out and threatened to tell the management unless . . .

'Unless I agreed to meet some friends she had – and – do things – with them – let them do things to me . . .'

I didn't ask what kind of things. I didn't really want to know. So Sylvia had tried to blackmail Belinda into joining a vice group and Belinda had refused point blank. From what Belinda could gather, Sylvia had already made some guarantee to the people she knew that she would get Belinda for them (they'd seen her at the disco) and when Belinda had said no, Sylvia had gotten mad and tried to force her out of the place and into a car. Belinda had run back to the dressing room. Sylvia had produced a gun. There'd been a struggle. Belinda had gotten hold of the gun and shot Sylvia. It was manslaughter, maybe even self-defence. I told her she had little to worry about if the cops believed her story. She didn't seem impressed.

'It's just my word,' she said. 'Nobody saw anything.'

'I believe you,' I told her. 'Why shouldn't the cops?'

'Even if I did, what about the jury?'

She had a point. I frowned.

'What if we could find some member of this group Sylvia mentioned?' I suggested. 'Someone who might testify that Sylvia had been commissioned to get you for them? That would convince anyone.'

Her lovely face brightened and was then depressed again. She shrugged. 'Nobody would come forward – who'd want to give that kind of evidence – admitting they were a member of a vice circle?'

She was right. I went to the closet and took my hat and coat out of it.

'Where are you going?' She grew alarmed again. The tears threatened.

'To see what I can dig up,' I told her. 'If we can't persuade a volunteer, I might be able to get something on this vice group and force someone to come forward. Stay here. If the cops ask me where you are, I'll have to tell 'em – but don't worry.'

I put a cigarette between my lips as I left. I lit it and paused outside the door. I was thinking what a fool I was. I was in trouble again; playing knight errant for some dame who could easily be making a sucker out of me. But I'd believed her. I wanted to help her. Maybe in the back of my mind I thought that if I did her a favour she might do me one. I'd fallen for that Alice in Wonderland innocence.

I went out to the rainy, neon-lit sidewalk and hailed a cab. I gave the address of The Black Room. The driver told me it was closed. I told him I knew that. It was ten after one in the morning and I was beginning to feel sour.

CHAPTER TWO

The Black Room was at basement and street level of a Southside block in a district that had been seedy but was becoming fashionable. Rain silvered the night in long streaks and the sidewalk was a strip of black ebony gleaming under the lamps. No cops to be seen. The body hadn't been found yet. It was Wednesday. I knew the discos generally closed early on Wednesdays. There was no-one in sight, just a few cars cruising by, their tyres hissing on the wet asphalt. I paid off the cab and went round to the back door which was marked STAFF. It was wide open, swinging in the wind. I walked through and found the dressing room. The lights were still on. I saw the body. Sylvia was dead all right, lying in a litter of clothes and make-up in the tiny dressing room. The big, black whip she used in her act lay near her, its thong curled around her upper calf.

She was tall, well-built, with lovely legs and firm flesh. She wasn't particularly young. Her long red hair was spread behind her head and her eyes were closed, her full mouth slightly open, as if to receive a lover's kiss. The only kiss she'd be getting now was from the skinny guy with the sickle who came to collect her wicked little soul.

Her arms were flung out at her sides and her legs were spread apart. She hadn't been wearing any underwear and the flimsy white dress had risen to her thighs, revealing her black garter belt. It wasn't sexy, any of it. It made me want to weep.

There was something dark and corrupt about her appearance, even in death. Just looking at her, without knowing her act, or knowing what she'd wanted from Belinda, you sensed she was a woman who revelled in perverse sexuality.

I didn't touch her. I started to search the room, hoping I could turn up some clue to the identity of Sylvia's 'friends'.

I found her purse and opened it. It contained the usual stuff — and one unusual item. I frowned, looking at the bronze badge and wondering how it came into the picture. It showed the Roman fasces — the bundle of sticks tied together that symbolised order and justice. The last people to use a badge like that had been Mussolini's Fascists! I thought of Mussolini. I thought of Italy. I thought of the Mafia. I thought of my old enemy Big Tuna Bastori, head of The Organisation, the local Mafia in these parts. I thought I was going crazy. Still holding the badge, certain that it was the clue I'd been looking for, I went to the phone and dialled the number of the Homicide Department.

I told them to put me through to Lieutenant Hunt.

Bill Hunt wasn't there. They asked me if I wanted to talk to anyone else. I said it could wait. I dialled Bill's home number and held on. I didn't have to hold on for more than a few rings. Bill's voice answered, alert as usual. He could come out of sleep in seconds. I told him the good news. He cursed me and said he'd come round. I said I'd be there.

As I turned, still fingering the little badge and wondering about it, hoping Bill could tell me something, the door opened and something glossy walked in.

The guy was in evening clothes, with brilliantined hair that outshone his patent leather shoes. He was about six feet two with a cleft chin and the good looks of a college football player. But the looks were deceptive. He must have been forty. The mouth had odd lines on it. The eyes were very hard. I knew the face. We'd printed it in the *Trib*'s gossip page before. It was Rudy Klosterheim of the Klosterheim millions. A big man in the Windy City. A powerful man who backed politicians and racketeers and similar deserving causes.

'Give me that badge,' he said.

'No,' I said.

'Don't be foolish,' he said.

'Who's foolish?' I said.

He chewed his lip. 'I'll buy it.'

'How much?'

'Five grand.'

I whistled. 'So it's worth five grand.'

'Only to me. Know who I am?'

'I do.'

'Don't cross me, chum,' he said.

'You know Sylvia's dead?' I asked politely, nodding towards the less-than-decorous corpse.

He didn't turn his head, but he took a gun from the pocket of his topcoat and he pointed it meaningfully at my stomach.

'So you knew,' I opined. 'And you came back for this? The old Fascist badge? What is it? The badge of the club you belong to – the one Sylvia tried to get Belinda for?'

'Oh, I'll enjoy killing *you*,' he said between clenched teeth.

'Go ahead,' I said. 'Wish I could enjoy the sight of the cops arriving just as you do it.'

'You called the police?' His voice became nervous. 'The local precinct?' He sounded as if he could handle the local precinct.

'Bill Hunt of Homicide,' I told him.

He put the gun away. 'You a cop?'

'I'm Beck of the *Trib*. I'm worse than a cop – I'm a fearless reporter. Tell me about your group, Mr Klosterheim. Can anyone join? Or is it exclusive? We'd like to do a story on it.'

'Write a word and I'll make sure you never write another,' he said.

'I was hoping for a more original quote.'

There was the sound of a siren and tyres squealing.

He left the dressing room in a hurry.

He must have managed to avoid Bill Hunt and his boys, because when they came in they didn't say anything about him. I decided I wouldn't say anything either. I put the little badge in my pocket. I felt Mr Klosterheim was the lead I needed.

Bill Hunt had that bitter look in his eyes that every cop wears when wakened in the middle of the night to come look at a corpse.

'How'd you find the body?' he asked, bending over Sylvia's cold, curved cadaver.

'Her killer told me where to look,' I said.

Bill straightened up. 'No games, Hank. The full story. Fast.'

I thought he might even hit me if I didn't tell him. I told him. When he'd listened he pursed his lips and looked around the room, finally fixing his eyes back on the corpse.

'You say you believe her?'

'I believe her,' I said. 'And I want to find some witness who'll verify her story.'

'You're crazy,' he said. 'Who'd—?'

'I'm going to find someone,' I broke in.

'In how many weeks?' Bill's mouth wore a sardonic tilt.

'Tonight,' I told him.

He shrugged. 'You try. We'll pick up the girl. She's at your apartment now?'

'That's where she is.'

'We'll go together,' Hunt said.

CHAPTER THREE

When we got there the apartment was bare and Bill gave me a long, hard stare.

I shrugged. 'Sorry.'

'Know where she'll be?'

'Her address will be at the discotheque, I guess.' I said.

He walked out of the apartment without a word. I had the feeling he didn't like me too much that night.

I gave him a couple of minutes while I hunted up a few things I might need for the excursion I planned, then I followed him out.

There were no cabs around. I began to walk. I was thinking of paying a call on Mr Rudy Klosterheim. As I turned the corner of the block, I heard footsteps behind me. I swivelled round. Three men stopped and looked at me. There wasn't any doubt that they wanted to see me. There wasn't much doubt that they'd been waiting for me. I was pretty sure of another thing – they wanted to do me violence.

Two were small, ratty-faced men with the look of cheap hoods. The other man was bigger, with the look of a cheap hood who was making money. He was the tough one. He was the one who snarled at me. I made out the words.

'Give us the badge you found at The Black Room.'

'Mr Klosterheim ask you to ask me?' I said politely.

'Just hand over the badge, baby,' said the big one.

'What if I don't?'

'We'll hurt you,' said one of the rat-faces.

'You don't look so tough,' I remarked.

They came at me then. I didn't bother too much with the little ones, but I kicked the big one's shin as he reached for me. It gave me time to slam the two little rats' heads together. I left them reeling about and got a good judo grip on big boy and let him push himself over my shoulder. He landed on the sidewalk with a solid sound. He stayed there. One of the rat-faces had drawn a knife. I chopped down on his wrist and he let go of the knife. I clipped him a short one on the jaw and he crumpled. I swung on the last member of the rough-up party and my fist dented his chin, too. They lay there in a heap. I walked away from there, stopped at the nearest phone, called the cops to pick up the three, called the local cab stand.

As the cab took me uptown, I saw the police wagon arrive.

I'd decided that I now had a personal score to settle with Mr Klosterheim. I was going to get him to be the witness Belinda needed. I was definitely going to get him.

CHAPTER FOUR

The Klosterheim house was big, ostentatious and glossy, like its owner. It had a wall around it, and gates, and the gates were closed. I told the cab to wait and I climbed over the gates and moved towards the house.

There was a light coming from the french windows at the back of the house.

I slunk towards the light and peeked in through a chink in the drapes.

Then I knew that Belinda hadn't gone home. She hadn't done anything on her own free will. I cursed myself for opening my mouth to Klosterheim too much. He must have realised who I was, found my address, sent his men around to pick up Belinda.

She was wearing the same pale green paisley trouser suit which she wore for her dancing act and which she'd worn to my apartment. She was sitting in a high-winged chair with Klosterheim standing over her holding his gun. There was a little bruise on the right side of her mouth. She looked very scared indeed. She looked like she needed protection. I felt protective. I drew my Colt and poised myself to kick in the windows, hoping I could do it with one kick. Just as I was ready, I saw a movement through the chink and had another look.

Klosterheim was pushing Belinda towards the door. I decided that since they were leaving the room I could be more subtle. I had the compact cracksman's tool kit that Hymie Janson had given me taped to my inner thigh. I could try a key on the door.

As I was going through the somewhat complicated routine of getting at the tool kit, I heard the front door slam.

Klosterheim must be taking the girl away somewhere.

I ran round the house in time to see him forcing Belinda into a big, restored Duesenberg, as ostentatious as everything else Klosterheim possessed.

I was desperate. I crept towards the gate and huddled in the shrubbery as Klosterheim drove the car up to the gate and, keeping Belinda covered with his gun, opened it to let the car through.

As soon as the car was gone, I signalled for my cab. It came smoothing up and I jumped in. I told him to follow the car.

We headed back downtown and were soon in the Southside district again. We saw the Duesenberg enter a narrow alley and douse its lights. I had a word with the cabby, paid him off and moved cautiously down the sidewalk until I reached the entrance to the alley. I peeked around the corner and saw Klosterheim shoving Belinda out of the car and through a doorway. A dead neon sign could be seen. It said PORTIA'S DISCOTHEQUE — MEMBERS ONLY. Chicago was full of discotheques since the boom had started the year before. Maybe I'd found the headquarters of the vice group Belinda had mentioned. If so, I had a scoop for the paper, the evidence I would need to support Belinda's story, or possibly the prospect of being found next morning floating face down in Lake Michigan.

It was still raining as I walked down the alley towards the club.

It wasn't raining bricks, though.

It was a brick that fell on my head.

Or something like a brick.

A gun butt or a blackjack, I figured later.

Whatever it was, it certainly put me to sleep. The world slid sideways, I slid downwards. Just then, I didn't much care what was happening.

When I woke up, the world was still swaying. I opened my eyes and turned my head and my head began to throb, throb, throb. It wasn't only my head, either. There was music – wild, Tamla Motown music turned to maximum volume. I saw bars, bright light above me from a central hanging chandelier, gold speckled wall beyond it. It looked like a discotheque in its decor. Then I realised what I was in.

I was in one of the cages they suspend over the floor for the girl to dance in. It was hanging from a couple of heavy, central cables from the ceiling.

I heaved myself to my feet, using the bars for support. The cage was swaying, its anchoring cables had been removed.

I looked down at the floor.

I closed my eyes.

When I opened them again I saw what I'd seen before and this time I looked longer.

Klosterheim was there and he wasn't wearing his monkey suit any more. He was clad in a pair of black tights and jackboots. Otherwise, he was naked. The girl who knelt before him – a big, heavy blonde in an attitude of supplication – was stark naked. Her head was thrown back and there was a yearning expression on her face.

In one hand, Klosterheim held a long, slender rod. He reached out with it and stroked it over the girl's face, breasts and stomach, caressingly. Her mouth opened and closed pleadingly. Her breasts heaved up and down. I felt sick.

Then, as I turned away, I saw something that made me feel worse.

It was Belinda, also completely naked; but she was spreadeagled, hanging from golden chains suspended, like the cage, from the roof. There were chains pulling her legs apart and anchored to the floor. Her stomach was about level with Klosterheim's head.

There were other people in the room – about a dozen men and women. I recognised faces. They were all top society people.

I knew I'd found the vice group, but there wasn't much I could do about it.

Klosterheim looked up then, and a big smile crossed his face.

'Hello, Mr Beck. Welcome to Portia's Discotheque. The floor show is about to begin. I thought you'd like to see it. You've got a great view.'

I didn't say anything. I didn't let him see any expression. I just stared at him hard. He shrugged, raised his rod and brought it down with a great thwack across the kneeling girl's back. She moaned and fell on her hands and knees to the floor in front of him. He started to whip her in time to the roaring music. I retched.

Below, the others were also beginning to leap around in time to the music, flailing at one another in an ecstasy of sado-masochistic glee.

Klosterheim stopped long enough to point his slender rod at Belinda and shout to me.

'You see, she finally let herself be persuaded to join us. She's going to die, Mr Beck. Can you guess how?'

Belinda moaned and writhed in the chains. My heart was full of pity for her and my mind was clouded with hatred for Klosterheim. The man was insane.

I grasped the slim metal bars. They weren't that thick, but they were too thick to bend with my bare hands. And they were too narrow to let me get out.

I had to do something.

I looked around. I saw the chandelier that gave light to the hall. I saw the sprinkler system above me on the ceiling. On the wall nearest me I saw the pipes that fed the system. At one point they curved in a U on their way down the wall. There seemed to be a gap between them and the wall.

A desperate idea was beginning to form in my sickened mind.

Klosterheim leapt forward and brought the rod down across the front of Belinda's thighs. She shrieked in agony. I couldn't take it. I had to try and go through with the plan, no matter how desperate it was.

I began to swing the cage from side to side as the music pounded on and the sick wretches below continued to perform their dreadful ritual.

Faster and faster I swung the cage, hoping that Klosterheim and his friends were too absorbed in their perverted activities to notice what I was doing.

Then I did it. The cage swung out and struck the chandelier with a great splintering of glass and sparks. The lights went out.

Still the music pounded, but below they had fallen silent.

There was still a little dim light from the single skylight window high above. It was all I needed to swing the cage in the opposite direction and claw out to catch the water pipe at the U-bend. My muscles strained and my whole body shook with agony as I managed to wedge one of the bars behind the pipe. Then I put my back to the cage and used my feet as a lever, trying to bend the bar outwards.

The pipe was creaking and, inch by inch, the bar began to bend.

When it happened, it happened suddenly.

The bar bent outwards and the water pipe came with it. Water began to gush from it on to the floor. That gave me another idea.

The cage was swinging free now, the bar bent enough to let me through. As it swung towards the light cable, I grabbed it as I passed and swung the cage harder until I was close to the gushing water.

Down below people were shouting and then I heard a gun bang.

'Stop it, Beck, whatever you're doing!' It was Klosterheim's voice. 'I'll shoot you Beck!'

I grabbed the twisted pipe, with the water coming out of it in a steady stream to the floor. Carefully, I touched the naked light cable to it.

I felt good, then. I heard them screaming. What I had done was to use the water to conduct the electricity to the floor and I was giving the people below a heavy shock. It wasn't enough to do them serious injury, but it was enough to give them something to think about. It stopped Klosterheim's shots.

Then what I knew would happen did happen. The electricity fused.

While they were still in confusion, I squeezed through the bars, hung for a moment, and then dropped to the water-sodden floor. Every light in the building was probably out of commission now.

I saw Klosterheim loom out of the gloom as I ran towards Belinda.

His face was a mask of hatred as he pointed the gun at me. I didn't stop to think. I just leapt at him. We both fell to the floor. He was still holding the gun.

We rolled about on the floor, grappling, as I tried to get the gun from his hand.

I felt someone else grab me. It made me even more desperate. I managed to free myself from Klosterheim and clipped him a short, hard punch on the jaw. It made him groggy. I got hold of the gun.

I stood up.

Now that my eyes were used to the gloom, I could see all the people standing around me, tensed. Some of their faces were full of fear. I think they guessed how the cookie was crumbling now.

I relaxed and grinned. I motioned with the gun.

'Bunch up,' I said, 'so you're all together.' I shoved Klosterheim, who was now on his feet, towards the rest of the perverted crew.

Nearby, Belinda was sobbing quietly. I waved the gun again and pointed at one of the naked women – the wife of a well-known local politician. 'Get her down,' I said.

As the woman helped Belinda to the ground, I decided there was one more thing I wanted to do.

I'd left a message with the cab-driver to fetch Bill Hunt and his men. They should be arriving soon.

I wanted to wrap up the job neatly, and I thought I knew how to do it.

CHAPTER SIX

When Hunt arrived, I'd managed to get the emergency power working.

He looked surprised as he saw what I'd prepared for him.

While waiting for him to arrive, I'd made the whole sick gang get into the cage, then I'd winched it up above the floor. They were all in there. The expressions on their faces went from stark fear at the knowledge that their careers and reputations were finished, to utter hatred (particularly on Klosterheim's face).

Belinda was beside me, wearing her trouser suit again. I had my arm around her. In my other hand I held the gun I'd taken from Klosterheim.

Bill couldn't keep his cool.

'For chrissakes, Hank, what *is* this?'

'All the evidence you need,' I said. 'There's the members of the vice group that tried to get Belinda. There's half-a-dozen major raps you can hand 'em. I don't think Belinda will have any trouble getting acquitted.'

Bill recovered.

'Why send for the Homicide Department,' he said sourly. 'This is a Vice Squad job, you know.'

I grinned at him. He grinned back.

Belinda hugged me tightly.

She was grateful.

Very grateful.

She showed me just how much for several nights that followed.

Oh, and of course, I had one of the hottest scandal scoops for the paper that the world-weary Windy City had ever known.

It got me a raise, even though the story didn't appear under my by-line.

But mainly it got me the gratitude of Belinda Fayre.

I wasn't complaining.

Sexton Begg's listeners were entertained by the story but their true curiosity concerned a very famous case which had occurred in the recent future. This odd tale, of murder and the supernatural, had filled the headlines for months and was still re-told in the press from time to time. It concerned a mysterious villain and a series of daring, cold-blooded murders which had caused the whole of London to lock its doors for those long months when a singular killer roamed abroad. It was thought he was the same as the monster who had terrorised Mirenburg in the last years of that city's independence. A bit of doggerel persists from those days, telling the story in the sensational language of the popular broadsheet . . .

8. crimson eyes

CHAPTER ONE

Crimes of the City

We are all familiar with the wave of murders, scandals and suicides coinciding with the collapse of BBIC and culminating on Christmas Eve with the bizarre death of a profoundly unpopular Prime Minister.

'That poor fellow captained the most incompetent crew of self-impressed scamps ever to tangle themselves in the rigging of the ship of state,' declared Sir Sexton Begg, heading the investigation. 'But, however apt, I wouldn't wish a fate like his on anyone.' A Callahan Home Office appointee, Begg had led the inquiry into the financial affairs of his own nephew, Barbican Begg, whose mighty frauds had drained the country.

Barbican himself had disappeared, but the aristocrats, politicians and famous plutocrats left to face trial made a sensational list, especially as they began to be killed. Barbican Begg himself had been married to the Prime Minister's sister Wendy, who had overdosed two years earlier. A certain coolness between the two men had not interfered with their association. The government depended heavily on Begg's help. It had continued to endorse BBIC while the cabinet gave authority to large-scale money laundering in the British Caribbean territories, for Begg was underwriting some of its most lunatic flotations.

The first murders in what soon emerged as a pattern had been discovered a year earlier, preceding Barbican Begg's exposure by months. At Marriage's Wharf, Wapping, three armed skinheads had been killed by a large blade leaving a single, identical wound which at first looked like the imprint of a pair of lips. The detective in charge believed the skinheads to have been slaughtered in self-defence.

KGB, he thought. There was something subtly Slavic about the method. A former MI5 man, given to unfashionable and over-subtle analysis, he could not easily explain the corpses' grotesque colour, nor the hideous terror marking the dead faces; unless, he suggested, the blade had been poisoned.

The pathologist brought in was a retired Scotland Yard man whom Begg had known in his private detective days. Dr 'Taffy' Sinclair's respect for Begg was returned. In the past, Dr Sinclair had discovered causes of death previously never imagined but was bound to admit bafflement in this case. 'Clearly they were all stabbed,' he told his old colleague over Christmas pints of foaming Ackroyd's at The Three Revenants, 'yet I couldn't swear they'd been stabbed to *death*.' The pathologist's high, pale forehead had creased in a frown. 'It's fanciful, Begg, but if you asked how they'd died I'd have to say – well – that something was *sucked* out of them. Not blood, especially. Not even their lives, really – something worse. And by some filthy means, too.' He shuddered.

Sexton Begg had inspected several victims. Long after the Marriage's case, a senior Lloyd's officer was discovered in a Streatham brothel. His costume had greatly excited the popular imagination but Begg had been impressed by his horrified expression, the peculiar silvery sheen of the skin, the bloodless wound like a kiss. Save for the wound's position, the Prime Minister had died in exactly the same way. 'As if their souls had been drained?' Begg ordered two more pints of Vortex Water.

Sinclair was enthusiastic. 'Quite. It's not the first time you and I have run up against so-called black magic, but this affair beats everything, eh? Witnesses?'

Begg had no useful witnesses. Those who had heard voices from the Prime Minister's sitting room could not tell if the other speaker was native or foreign. Someone had glimpsed what he described as a 'stained-glass window' full of every imaginable colour which seemed to take the shape of a jewelled cup, its gold and silver blazing so powerfully he was almost blinded before it vanished. The piteous, blood-curdling cry awakened Downing Street at 4am. Someone heard the front door close. Sleeping soldiers and police outside were discovered unhurt. 'But I'm seeing two chaps tomorrow morning who sound better. One claims he spotted the murderer leaving BBIC on the night in question, when most of Barbican's closest associates called a crisis meeting at their HQ and were identically murdered. Noises – like music or singing – and a brilliant glow were reported, but the assassin was invisible. I gather my first witness believes he saw the Devil.'

Begg added: 'I have rarely felt so thoroughly in the presence of the Supernatural. Rationally, we must assume this is a clever murderer using superstition to terrify his victims in advance, enabling him to kill them without any significant resistance. That night he murdered 14 of the City's cleverest men, including Sir John Sheppard, Lord Charles Peace, Duval of the Credite Lyonesse, Thomas King, Ricky Turpin and all three Al Glaouis. Only a day later he killed a whole school of Wall Street sharks over here in similar haste – Bass, Floyd, Cassidy, J W Harding, the James brothers, Schultz, the Bush boys and several others, equally renowned. Not a bad score.'

'You don't suggest this chap's done the world a favour?'

'Those who feed like parasites upon their fellows pretty much deserve to have the life sucked out of them, I'd say. The amounts of laundered crack money alone were obscene. This business sickens me, old man. Cabinet ministers are dying faster than they can resign. I've no love of the vigilante, but I cannot say I mourn the rascals' passing. My chief regret is that they did not die with their Swiss account numbers branded on their foreheads.'

Begg's uncharacteristic pronouncements surprised Sinclair. 'You seem to have more sympathy for the assassin than his prey.'

'Absolutely true,' Begg agreed. 'Believe me, Taffy, it's my very sympathy which should soon bring me face to face with our murderer!'

CHAPTER TWO

An Interview with Lady Ratchet

The Prime Minister had not been the only politician to die violently on Christmas Eve. Over in Limehouse, in identical circumstances, while his wife and children were at church praying for his mediocre soul, the education minister, Horace Quelch, was discovered at the centre of a pentacle, not part of the seasonal decorations, designed to save him from the demon he believed he had summoned.

Sexton's first witness claimed to have bumped into the murderer as he was leaving Eel House, Quelch's 18th-century merchant's mansion. There were only two entrances to Eel House – the first from the river, the second from a low gate into an apparently dead-end alley where 'Corky' Clarke, a small-time sneak-thief, had been as he put it 'catching his breath' in the heavy fog so characteristic of London since the repeal of the Clean Air Act. Hearing a soft movement behind him, he had turned to see what he first took to be two disembodied eyes . . .

'Red and troubled as the flames of Hell, Sir Sexton. Coming out of that evil, muddy fog. I swear, I hadn't had a drop.' Corky's ginbloated features contradicted his claim, but Begg was inclined to believe him. It was Boxing Day. They sat together in Begg's rather austere morning room at Sporting Club Square where pale light, filtering through old lace, gave the room a silvery, rather unreal, appearance.

Clarke had glimpsed bone-white skin 'like a leper's', a dark cape revealing a scarlet lining and the hilt of a massive sword in black, glowing iron, set with a huge ruby. 'I thought he must be the Devil, Sir Sexton. You would have done, too. He came at me so sudden and horrible! His eyes pulled my heart out of my chest and left me gasping, tasting that sharp, oily fog as if it was the sweetest air of Kent, and so grateful for my life! I heard his footsteps, light and bright like a woman's, tapping off up Salt Pie Passage. Oh, Lord, sir! I never want to endure that again. I thought all my sins had caught up with me. Those crimson eyes! I'm a new man now, sir, and conscience-bound to answer your poster.'

'Mr Clarke, you've done well and I commend you!' Sexton Begg was excited. 'You bring to mind an old neighbour of mine!' Corky's description had triggered a train of thought Begg was anxious to pursue. 'I note you've joined Purity Bottomley's Born Again Tolstoyans and work for the relief of the homeless. Good man!' He pressed a couple of 'shields' into the fellow's palm.

'God bless you, Sexton Begg!'

'It's you, Mr Clarke, God will surely bless! Soon all Britain will have reason to thank you. Farewell, my good chap. I must shortly interview my next witness.' And with a flourish Begg opened the door for the reformed crook, telling Mrs Curry to preserve his peace at all costs for the next hour. Whereupon he went immediately to his shelves, selecting a large German quarto, a jar of his favourite M&E and a baroque meerschaum. Reading eagerly he flung himself down at his table, his pipe already forgotten. Begg was smiling thoughtfully to himself when Curry announced his next visitor.

Hamish Ogilvy worked as a porter-attendant at the New Billingsgate Fish Museum. Still in his uniform, he was a small, eager man with a soft Highland accent. On special leave, he was clearly in awe of the famous Sexton Begg as the investigator kindly coaxed his story from him . . .

On the night of the BBIC murders, Ogilvy, staying late in attendance on a pregnant cuttlefish, had missed the evening bus and decided to risk the walk to Liverpool Street. There was another fog and Ogilvy was soon lost, arriving at last in Crookburn Street at the corner of Sweetcake Court where BBIC's brutal architecture was softened by the weather. Pausing to read a sign, he heard a cab behind him. Hoping to ask his way, he saw the cab had come for a shady figure hurrying from BBIC. 'I saw her face through the taxi window, Sir Sexton. She was staring back, terrified out of her skin. It was that poor, loony Mrs Ratchet, who used to be in the government. Pale as a ghost. I could almost hear her teeth chattering.'

Ogilvy was also rewarded and thanked, though less enthusiastically. Reluctantly, Begg decided to follow up the account. Apart from Barbican Begg, Lady Ratchet was the only surviving BBIC director. Under the impression that she was variously the English Queen, the Israeli Prime Minister, the American President and Mary, Queen of Scots, she was at best an unreliable witness. She had moved South of the River on the assumption that her enemies could not cross running water and refused all visitors, even relatives. She went out only to 'go over my books'. She did not trust modern electronics so her accountants kept a large ledger which she inspected every month. She agreed to a telephone interview only after Begg threatened, under his new powers, forcible entrance of her Esher Tudor castle.

Gentle and firm as possible with the babbling old creature, Begg believed a small, cunning and perfectly coherent mind lay beneath 'interference' designed to bully and exhaust opposition. Steadfastly he refused her threats, whines, pathetic lies and claims and continued to demand an account of her whereabouts on the night of the murders. 'Nonsense,' she insisted, 'I was never there. I was not very well that evening. A touch of Alzheimer's. My doctor will swear to it. I was at the pictures. Whoever you saw, it wasn't me. An imposter. You'd better question your chum Elizabeth. She never liked me. They were after the cup, too, you know. They said it was theirs by right. Poppycock! They knew how much it was worth. We planned to set up an office in York. But it's not safe there any more.'

Begg insisted he meet her and talk 'chiefly for your own protection'. Eventually he persuaded her, by wonderfully veiled threats, to meet him or be arrested for murder.

'Very well, Sir Sexton.' She was suddenly brisk. 'I respect your family name. Be ready to receive me this evening at six o'clock in Sporting Club Square. But please be prepared also to take responsibility for your actions . . .'

'I am very grateful, Lady Ratchet. By the by, would you try to recall on your way if you ever knew a fellow by the nickname of "Crimson Eyes"?'

There was a cold pause. At length Lady Ratchet replaced the receiver.

CHAPTER THREE

The last victim

Heavy snow was falling. The Boxing Day sun had set over Sporting Club Square. Lady Ratchet, mad as she was, had never been late. Begg went to his sitting room windows and pulled back the rich, tawny Morris curtains on which the firelight made a new, dancing geometry. He peered through the blackness, through the big white flakes, through the sharply defined branches of plane trees, down into the square, towards the elaborate iron gates where 'Mad Maggie' would enter.

At three minutes to six he was sure he heard a taxi setting down. Since then, save for the occasional muffled stamping of snow-laden feet, the Square had grown silent. Glancing again at his gleaming Tompion, Begg saw that it was four minutes past the hour. At that moment, the soft winter air was pierced by the high-pitched shriek of a police whistle. Begg started, as if struck by a new idea, and hurried to don his overcoat. He reached the policeman outside the gates in less than a minute. 'What's up, officer?'

The answer lay before them, already touched by a thickening layer of snow. The frail, twisted little body Begg instantly recognised from the shoes subtly clashing with the skirt. It was poor old 'Mad Maggie'. Noting the black leather trophy case in her left hand, Begg knelt beside the body, feeling uselessly for a pulse. The corpse seemed to shrivel as he watched, as if it had been animated solely by its owner's lunacy. Her face stared up at him through snow still melting on her fading paint. It was an expression of unmitigated terror. There was no sign of a wound. Maggie Ratchet had died clutching at her own throat. Who had known she was on her way to see him?

Begg looked around for footprints. The snow had already obscured the trail. By the way she lay half in the gutter and half on the pavement, Lady Ratchet had met her death as she entered the square.

'By God, sir,' exclaimed the policeman. 'It's like she ran into Jack the Ripper and Mr Hyde at the same time. What do you think she saw, sir?'

'Oh, I'd guess something much worse than either,' said Sexton Begg.

CHAPTER FOUR

Old blood

It was one in the morning, Boxing Day over, and snow continuing to fall. Begg, wrapped in a heavy Ulster and fur cap, stood in the darkness of an archway on the third floor of a Sporting Club Square mansion only five blocks from his own. Begg's stoicism was famous, but tonight he felt his age. At last he heard a soft footfall in the snow outside. A door opened almost silently. Light steps sounded on the carpeted stairway and at last a tall figure in full evening dress appeared on the landing, stepping forward with a latch-key held out in its bone-white hand.

It was then that Begg revealed himself.

'And did you enjoy the Messiaen, monsieur?'

A death's head whirled round to confront him. The eyes were covered with thick, round tinted lenses, as if sensitive to the faintest light. Gauntly handsome features showed amusement as Begg struck a match to reveal his own face.

'The Messiaen had its moments, you know,' said the albino. 'But the English play French music impossibly badly. Good evening, old neighbour. You see I'm back in my chambers. We last met in Mirenburg when you were trying to draw up a treaty to stop the Serbian border wars. You didn't know about your government's substantial arms interest. I think you were right to resign.'

With a movement of his head Begg let his old adversary open the door. A small oriental man appeared to take their outer garments, showing them into a sparsely furnished Japanese sitting room.

'A drink, Sir Sexton?' The albino removed his dark glasses to reveal crimson orbs whose strange light threatened to reach into Begg's very being and draw out his immortal soul.

'If you still keep that Armagnac, Count Ulrich, I would love some.' Begg's own eyes held steady, meeting the albino's.

'I'll join you!' To his servant: 'Bring the St Odhran Armagnac. Well, Sexton Begg, explain this small-hours melodrama!'

'You know my interest in the histories of our family's various branches and my special fascination with our common Central European ancestors. If you would spare me a little time, I would tell you a story?'

'Late as it is, Sir Sexton, I'm always glad to listen to your yarns. A detective tale, is it?'

'Nothing less. It concerns an event frequently recorded in poetry, plays, novels and films all across that part of Europe where Slav meets German. Perhaps you recognize this doggerel?

"A call to the Cautious, a Word to the Wise;
Tonight's the Night when Crimson Eyes,
His face bone-white and his Mouth blood-red,
Disdains the Body, but tastes the Head."'

Count von Bek laughed easily. 'Some *Rauber und Ritter* nonsense?

It means nothing to me. I have never been, as you have, fascinated by the patois and doggerel of the streets, Sir Sexton.'

'The poem's from Mirenburg.' Accepting a glass from the servant, Begg paused to enjoy its aroma. 'Your family's real home for centuries. Until Wäldenstein was absorbed into Austria, then Germany and then Czechoslovakia, the Saxon von Beks played a pretty important part in local politics. The legend I know from German literature is "Karmesinangen". The French called him Le Loup Blanc. Your family is closely associated with that and several other enduring Middle European legends.

'A recurrence of albinism is said to come every two generations, through the maternal line of Lady Rose Perrott, kinswoman to Anne Boleyn, who married Count Michael von Bek in 1560 in Mirenburg and gave birth to albino twins, Ulrich and Joachim. It's believed the albino line goes back before Attila, before the Romans, but like the story of your family's special affinity with the Holy Grail and a black sword carved with living runes, it is comparatively recent. The event on which the poem is based is from 1895 when Mirenburg was terrorised by a sequence of appalling murders. The victims were slain by a sword making a singular wound and leaving horrified corpses oddly coloured. A group of Rosicrucian exiles had got hold of a jewelled cup they claimed was the Holy Grail and summoned a demon to help celebrate an unholy ritual. The "demon", drawn some say from Hell itself, was none other than a revived Count Ulrich von Bek, otherwise known as "Crimson Eyes", whose lifespan is far longer than a common mortal's, thanks to his sword . . .

'Not a demon at all, but an avenging angel! It is the von Beks' duty to defend the Grail at all costs. Mirenburg legends say the family has a destiny to achieve the resolution of God and Satan.' Begg savoured his Armagnac.

'Old folk tales, Sir Sexton. How people love to chill their blood! So much more mysterious and romantic than the prosaic truth! Regrettably, we have little time to chat further. I'm off on my travels tomorrow.'

'I would imagine your business here is over,' agreed Begg. 'There's talk Barbican fled to the Caymans.'

'By coincidence, exactly where I'm bound, Sir Sexton.' The albino drew a case from his jacket and offered Begg a thin, brown cigarette, taking one for himself when the investigator refused. 'I'm growing too soft for these London winters.'

'The tale continues,' Begg went on equably. 'It seems a City and Wall Street consortium came by an old von Bek family heirloom mislaid in 1943 when the Nazis arrested the count in Mirenburg. A Polish officer sold a cup which, it was said, could heal or even raise the recently dead! The potential profit from such a thing was enormous. But it would only display its powers in the presence of Barbican Begg, its steward, who tried to sell his interests to shore up BBIC. Well, as you know, members began to die pretty regularly, first in ones and twos, then by the boardroom-full. Every man who helped set up the vast BBIC fraud was being wiped out. In 1895 the Mirenburg press noted that Crimson Eyes never killed a woman, a child or an innocent. Crimson Eyes could not kill old Lady Ratchet. He let her run away and eventually cross the river into Esher. Her poor, baffled brain was addled once and for all. She locked herself up.

Ironically, she had nothing to fear from Crimson Eyes. Neither she nor I knew that the von Beks had kept their Sporting Club Square flat. She ran into you while she was leaving her taxi and you were trying to catch it, because you were late for a supper concert at the Wigmore Hall. You did not even recognise her! But she knew you. She saw your eyes. She thought she had met her nemesis and she died of shock. Or, you might say, she died of guilt . . .'

Trained to hide his feelings, Count von Bek could not suppress a slight, sardonic smile. With a sigh, he sat back in his chair, his moody red eyes staring thoughtfully into the amber of the glass. 'So it's done at last. Apart from your nephew, of course, who seems to have taken the cup with him. I had not realised he was still in England until last week.'

'Hiding at Lady Ratchet's. She'd grown to resent him. He believed she'd betray him. If he has the cup, you, presumably, have the sword?'

'A grotesque old family relic, really. Would you like to see it?' The albino's voice had taken on a peculiar edge.

'That would be a privilege.' Begg's own voice was steady as steel. Rising, von Bek swiftly crossed the room to open a door in the wall. From within came a distant murmuring, like swarming bees. Von Bek stooped into the space and withdrew an ornate broadsword, scabbarded in heavily worked leather. A huge sphere in the hilt glowed red as the slender albino came to stand before Begg with the long scabbard stretched upon both white palms. 'There's our famous Mittelmarch blade, cousin. A rather rococo piece of smithery, you'll recall.'

'Perhaps you could slip it from the scabbard?' Begg suggested evenly.

'Of course.' Frowning, von Bek changed his grip and drew out a few inches of the blade. His arm shook violently. Now the sound became an angry muttering, horribly alien. Sexton realised he looked upon a living thing. There was something foully organic about the black metal within which red words swarmed – words in an alien alphabet Begg had seen only once before on three broken obsidian tablets buried in a tomb below a temple in Angkor Wat. Those runes bore no resemblance to anything else on Earth and Begg could not free his eyes from them. He was in their power. Inch by inch, the blade slipped from its scabbard, taking control of the creature who held it.

Then, with an enormous effort of will, Begg broke from his trance to shout: 'No! For the love of God, von Bek! Master your sword, man!'

He stepped back, watching as the albino, his red eyes blazing in their deep sockets, battled with the blade until at last he had resheathed it and fell exhausted back into his chair, as the sword muttered and shrieked in thwarted lust.

'It would have taken your soul,' said vok Bek coolly, 'and fed me my share.'

'I reminded myself of that,' said Begg. 'I know the secret of your longevity. We have the murder weapon, eh? The chief motive was retribution. And we know the method. Barbican and company needed your experience when the Grail stopped "working". You were invited to London and came ashore at Marriage's Wharf. As you realised what BBIC were up to, you took it upon yourself to "balance the books". I can't say I approve.'

'You have evidence for any of this?' Von Bek lit another drugged cigarette.

'The blade doubtless matches the wounds, but I'm not sure we want to release it into the world, do we? You are right, Count. I am unable to arrest you. But it has given me considerable satisfaction to solve this case and confront, as I had hoped, such an unusual killer. At a stroke or two you have considerably improved the probity of politics and business in this country. Yet, still, I disapprove of such actions.' He would not shake the pale hand when it was offered.

With a regretful shrug, Count Ulrich turned away. 'Differing times and cultures refuse us a friendship. Can I offer you some more of the St Odhran?'

But Begg, oddly depressed, made his excuses and left.

Returning home through the old year's snows, he reflected that, while one act of barbarism did not justify another, he could not, in his heart, say that this had been an unrewarding Christmas. He looked forward to returning to the warmth of his own fireside, of opening the black trophy case Lady Ratchet had brought him, to stare with quiet ecstasy into that blazing miracle of confirmation, that great vessel of faith and conscience: that Grail, of which he was now the only steward.

It seemed that story was half-familiar, at least to one of the company, who smiled at his niece across the great copper table, which stood at the centre of the Coffee Hall, and reminded her of their adventures in North Africa, in the days before the Arab world had united into two mutually supportive political unions, reconciled itself with Israel and become the envy of the West . . . 'I think I know the fellow you're talking about,' said Albert Begg. 'I had occasion to run across him more than once when I was seconded to the Foreign Office all those years ago, trying to be a diplomat. Of course I knew all the family legends – the grail and the sword and so on – but I had always rather assumed the stories to be tall ones, aimed at increasing the family mystique, especially in Germany and Middle Europe . . .'

9. no ordinary christian

CHAPTER ONE

Visitors to the City

He rode down from the Far Atlas with a corpse across his saddle and red hatred in his eyes. He had come out of a desert to reach the mountains. His blonde camel was quite mad, fearing only her rider, the albino aristocrat 'Le Loup Blanc', who fought like a Berber and thought like a Jew.

Even Th'amouent's Caliph, Al Hadj Mou'ini al A'aid, that ogre of self-indulgent cruelty, the shame of Islam, treated Le Loup Blanc with wary respect, and there were orders abroad to let him go freely. For this was no ordinary Christian.

This was one who spoke the purest Arabic of the Mosque, could joke in the coarse, rich Marakshi dialect, converse readily in all the Berber tongues or tell a tale in Egyptian which would make you think him a native of Alexandria or Cairo. Yet he let them call him by no name save his own, though he prayed with every sign of quiet devotion, five times a day.

They must address him in the Christian fashion as Fan Bekh, Al Rique, Bin Basha, but had no idea why anyone would willingly go by such an unholy string of gibberish. Out of respect they called him this to his face, but behind his back they called him Al Rik'h, The Secret One, in the familiar dialect of the Western Rif.

His lips were raw, his eyes dusty as uncut rubies, his white hair caked with the desert's grime. Though he wore the hooded djellaba of the Berberim, it had not protected his strangely unpigmented skin, which now flaked like a leper's so it seemed Death himself came riding through the ochre gates of Th'amouent on that May evening, with a crimson sun falling behind the blue mountains and the quarter moon bringing clear light to silver streets and the golden domes of mosques, to blue-tiled towers and time-worn terracotta. At that moment the muezzin began to chant. It was like a scene, said Captain Albert Begg, peering from his balcony through dark green palms below, from his favourite Rimsky Korsakov opera, *Manfred; or, The Gentleman Houri*. Had his visitor seen it in London when he was last there?

'Sadly, the old country's given me my marching orders.' Captain Quelch sighed. The hatchet-featured European wore a rather crumpled white dinner jacket and had undone his tie. 'So much for *non nobis sed omnibus*, eh, sport? You said you sold aeroplanes. Any particular type?'

'Well, it's not really aeroplanes,' Begg admitted. 'It's more general ordnance and that sort of thing.'

'Don't be embarrassed, old boy.' Quelch brightened up and again helped himself from Begg's decanter. He was making the most of the single malt. His hands were scarcely shaking at all. He winked a bloodshot eye. 'I've run a few guns to a few dusky customers in my time. Damned rum chap though, ain't he, that German? Prince what's-his-name? I've seen him before.'

'Like a knight of old,' said Poppy Begg, taking a poetic sip of her gin. 'Like Arthur's paladin upon a quest.' She rustled her pretty silk. 'He doesn't look happy.'

Captain Quelch cleared his throat. 'Neither would you, dear, if you'd just come in from the desert with a three-day-old corpse under your nose.'

'It could be a dead friend,' Poppy offered, anxious to keep the air of romance alive. Boyishly groomed in the very latest London fashion, she was already completely enchanted by the city and its blue-veiled Taureq, its lively mixture of Arab traders and Berbers, of bustling camels, donkeys and the occasional motor-car. Her uncle had decided to bring her with him on this official trip because it was a better alternative to what she would do if he had left her alone at his Sporting Club Square flat. Poppy felt obliged to be wild. It won her the approval of her peers. Albert Begg had, he believed, never met such an appalling gang of wastrels and scallywags and the thought of even one of them crossing his threshold, especially when he was not there, had been too much to bear.

'He probably has a habit of bringing in every poor little benighted coon who wanders too far away from camp,' suggested Captain Quelch. 'I wonder what his game is? Is there a reward for that sort of thing?' He frowned and let a small, gentlemanly belch escape his lips.

'You must tell me when we meet up again, old soul. I'll be on my way out of here by tomorrow.' He patted his jacket. 'The sooner I can cash this draft at the Credite Lyonesse in Marrakech, the happier I'll be. He's a bit of an unreliable customer, our Caliph, as I think you know.'

'I've still to meet him,' said Albert Begg, 'but I've had reports.' He did not wish Captain Quelch to know that he was here on government business and if his old acquaintance wished to believe he was in the same trade, running guns and tanks into North Africa, it suited him.

Begg's papers introduced him to the Caliph and requested safe passage, but his real purpose here was to meet the man who had just ridden through the Hakhim Gate. So far, an audience with the Caliph, who had a short attention span and a murderous impatience, had not taken place. Begg was confident, however, that his special status as His Majesty's Courier protected both himself and his niece – especially since the Caliph, in one of his most Byzantine schemes, was currently attempting to win British or German support against the French, who were threatening his autonomy. This consideration would last long enough, Begg believed, for him to achieve his mission and return with Poppy to Marrakech, where he could entrain immediately for Casablanca and a navy cruiser waiting in the quarantine harbour to take him home.

'He's my kinsman, I understand,' Albert Begg said of von Bek. 'The German side of the family was always of a romantic disposition. I put this chap's problems down to reading too much Karl May as a boy. Look what happened to old Lawrence. G A Henty as good as murdered him with his bare hands. That kind of fiction isn't healthy for a literal-minded dreamer. Conrad knew. But you can't help feeling that the world's a better place for the likes of our romantic lunatics, wouldn't you say, Quelch?'

'Lock the blighters up and throw away the key, old boy. That's my opinion. They do too much damage. Just think of the chaos Shelley alone has caused in the world! I'm a believer in old-fashioned values when it comes down to particulars. Strict discipline, that's my motto. I was always a good master, you know. The lascars respect a bit of firmness. They loved me, those boys.'

'Von Bek's life doesn't make you envy him or want to meet him?'

'I'm sorry, old chap, but I'm rather more fastidious than some, I can't stand fleas. The Kraut's forever in and out of those tents and native hovels. Imagine how infested he must be. No, no, old boy – I'll forego the pleasure until he's had a couple of good carbolic baths.'

'Well,' said Captain Begg suddenly, 'I'm off for my evening stroll. I'll walk you home, Captain.'

'No need, old soul. I'll just drift down into the bar for a bit. They stay open to residents and I'll give 'em your room number, if you don't mind. Not to worry, my boy. I'll pay cash when it comes to the reckoning.'

And with that, Captain Quelch bowed to Poppy, kissed her uncertain hand, and departed. When Captain Begg went down a few minutes later, the old pirate had disappeared.

Captain Begg was not to witness the arrival of Le Loup Blanc at the vividly painted ornamental gates of the Caliph's palace, and would only hear later how the man he knew as Prince Ulrich von Bek would dismount carefully from his camel and lay the corpse upon the steps, crying out that the God of us all would demand justice for this profoundly wicked murder, and that Al Rik'h of the Forbidden Desert was even now on his way to the mosque to seek guidance and discover if he were to be God's instrument in the matter. If so, the white-faced one promised, he would return in due course to complete his business. It was as though the Lord of Hades himself led his snarling mount back into the gathering darkness of the medina.

When inspected, the corpse was found to be that of a young woman. In death her angelic face was at rest. It was impossible to understand how she could look so seraphic when the rest of her skin had been systematically flayed from her body.

Hearing of the incident, the Caliph ordered the woman's remains to be brought to him. He stared for some time at her, giving her far more attention than he gave most living creatures, particularly women, then eventually shrugged and ordered the corpse disposed of in the usual way. But those who had dared lift their eyes to glance at him noticed that he was disturbed, perhaps even afraid. When, however, his vizier asked if he should increase the guard on the gates, the Caliph was dismissive. 'What have I to fear from Al Rik'h? If Allah truly speaks to him, then Allah will advise him of the folly of setting himself against me. I have soldiers. He has only himself. I am, after all, a true Fathamid, carrying the blood of our Prophet in his veins.' This was more a political claim than an exact statement of truth. The Caliph's forefathers, boasting the blood of Fathima, the Prophet's daughter, to be theirs, had seized power in Th'amouent during a period when their predecessors, declaring themselves Sharifians (also of the Prophet's blood) were self-confidently decadent. In such matters, lacking any form of constitutional law, it was usual to make the claims of blood. Yet the Caliph spoke with his usual authority and it was generally supposed that he and the Secret One would go about their affairs without further confrontation, honour having, as it were, been put into the hands of God. There remained, nonetheless, a considerable amount of speculation. Where had Al Rik'h found the body and why had the discovery so angered him? Why had he assumed the flaying to be the Caliph's work? Why would he, who usually avoided public notoriety, make such a speech for all to hear? Who, anyway, was the dead girl?

And would Le Loup Blanc be back from the mosque to demand entry to the palace and satisfaction from the Caliph? asked a few. It was agreed that not even the Secret One would be the winner in such an encounter.

In all events, having spent the entire night in the mosque, Le Loup Blanc took part in the morning prayer, rolled up his mat and stepped outside to put on his elegant riding boots then mount his camel, who was now rested and not quite as inclined to charge and bite any passer-by who caught her disgusted eye. She was a magnificent white camel, worth at least twelve thousand dirhams, and dressed richly enough to rival the most dandified Taureq. Such beasts were rare this side of the Atlas, though bred for their own use by the wild Berberim of the Low Sahara, who had never had a reason to venture this far and no desire to trade their beasts for the trinkets of Th'amouent.

A few loafers followed the camel, asking questions of the owner, which he ignored. They admired it as their European counterparts would admire a Lamborghini and they conferred romance and admiration upon the owner in recognition of his power and his taste. They wondered amongst themselves if Al Rik'h would lead his camel back to the gates of the Caliph's palace. They were denied further excitement, however. The crimson-eyed one took the Sari-al-dhar, where the market stalls were being set up for the day's business, and stabled his camel behind the Restaurant Salaman Rushd', which he entered from the rear to take a glass of mint tea and break his fast. Relaxing in his chair on the verandah he watched Th'amouent go about her business like any local lounger enjoying the pleasure of others' activity, until Captain Albert Begg sat down beside him and ordered a café complait.

'Good morning, Captain,' said the Secret One softly, in German. 'I regret our time together is limited. This new business is a bad one and I must give it all my attention.'

Rapidly, Captain Begg extended his government's compliments and relayed its intelligence that Caliph Mou'ini, requiring distractions for a variety of reasons, was planning an expansion of his power into the mountains and beyond. His majesty was anxious to stop such an expansion and sought Prince Ulrich's help.

After some thought, Ulrich von Bek said that the assistance of the British Government in this matter would, he believed, be unnecessary. However, he appreciated its concern and assured it that should he ever require help in the region, he would call upon it at the first opportunity.

Amused by this courteous snub, Captain Begg bid his acquaintance good-morning and returned to his hotel. He had decided that the style of his report must be positive, in order to make up for the vagueness of its content.

CHAPTER TWO

The Forbidden Desert

There were a hundred tales told of 'Crimson Eyes' across the whole of Europe and most of Africa. The tales added supernatural powers to his undoubted natural gifts, and all were curious as to why he would choose the desert and the wild hills of the Atlas to live. Some scholars believed he might be imitating the Nazarene who, he insisted, was still his master. All were baffled, if this were the case, for in every other respect Al Rik'h appeared a model of Islam.

'There is a pain worse than giving up one's own life,' said Th'amouent's local philosopher, the tailor, Al Fezim, as he and Captain Begg sat taking coffee together in the D'Jemaa al Jehudim, the Square of the Jews, 'and that is the pain of losing a friend or someone of your own blood. That is why I wonder at such a miserable sacrifice on your prophet's part. Nothing, for instance, compared to what Abraham was prepared to do. Certainly, self-sacrifice in pursuit of one's faith can be a noble thing, but the loss of one's first-born is worse.'

'And that is what we could be said to imitate,' Albert remarked, smiling, 'not Christ's act of self-sacrifice, but God's.'

'You Christians are as subtle as Jews sometimes,' Al Fezim shook his head. 'We simple Muslims will never fathom you, I fear.'

Those familiar with the tales of Al Rik'h noted that his black companion was not with him. He was said to travel with a giant, Lobangu, who claimed to be an exiled chief of the Zulu and had sworn one day to reclaim his homeland from the Dutch invaders.

Ulrich von Bek, the Secret One, remained in Th'amouent for several more hours, contriving to come unnoticed to Captain Begg's chambers where they discussed certain secret business. Captain Begg was surprised by the visit. He had assumed his interview with Prince von Bek concluded. But the Prince asked a number of pertinent questions concerning British attitudes to the region and seemed satisfied. Then he was introduced to Poppy Begg who was naturally obsessively curious but reluctant to ask questions which would irritate him or cause him to leave. She was anxious for his approval.

When Ulrich von Bek rode his white camel out through the ochre gates of Th'amouent, he still left a city noisy with speculation. He had taken no further action against the Caliph, but had said nothing of future vengeance. He left a tension behind him and a mystery. Ascetic, handsome and alien, he had proved impossibly attractive to Poppy Begg.

For a little while the Caliph considered having Al Rik'h followed, but then thought better of it. Meanwhile Poppy had impulsively hired a fearless boy as her guide and, on horseback, had trailed the albino out of the city and into the hills.

By the evening, when the deep green shrubbery hung upon the limestone, casting rich shadows over the grey-brown rock, and gorgeous orange streamers poured across a dark blue sky, they had entered a narrow gorge which opened into the steep T'Chou Pass and Poppy found herself in utter blackness, the sky obscured by looming shelves of limestone. Unsure whether to camp or to press on, she trusted to her luck and by morning had led herself and the boy to the crest of the pass – where she was rewarded with a distant view of the blonde camel and her magnificent rider moving down toward the near-desert.

It was at this point, however, that the boy discovered an adult prudence, received half his fee, a horse and her good wishes, and headed back for home. With Al Rik'h well in sight, she plunged optimistically in his wake.

On the second night, half-crazed from heat and lack of sleep, she began to panic. She decided to camp. She dismounted and lost her horse immediately. She sat down on a rock and wept. Then she cursed. Then she got up and plunged on into the night, hoping to come upon her horse by chance in that narrow pass.

By morning, she had reached the floor of the desert and saw the tall albino beneath a palm tree, stamping out his fire and saddling his camel. Her horse was nearby, chewing on the rough grass.

Al Rik'h waited, poised in amusement, as she approached.

'Don't be angry,' she pleaded. 'I know it was awfully rude and deadly bad form to follow you like that, but my curiosity got the better of my manners. All I can do is apologise – and throw myself on your mercy.'

Already hooded and veiled in the Taureq fashion, the tall German regarded her from deep-set crimson eyes which were not without irony. 'Then I suppose I must forgive you,' he said. 'But what am I to do with you? I have an urgent appointment. It cannot wait. I suppose I must take you with me. Your horse is refreshed and ready for mounting. I propose you sleep in your saddle as we ride. I will show you how.'

With a cord about her waist and pommel, Poppy did in fact sleep through most of the afternoon with the mysterious nobleman relaxing on his own mount and leading hers.

That night he lit a fire and made them comfortable, preparing a soup from ingredients in his saddlebags which would not have been out of place at La Lapine Russe in Paris.

She was entranced by him and begged him to tell her how he had come to this life of hermitage in the far desert.

Prince Ulrich was surprisingly frank. Clearly, he was anything but a misanthrope. His need for isolation had nothing to do with dislike of his fellow creatures. His very openness further made him the object of Poppy's curiosity.

It was an old, familiar story, he said. Even as it was happening, he was aware of its venerable antiquity. Like others of his family, who were Saxons from Bek, he had taken up residence at the family home in Mirenburg, capital of Wäldenstein, the loveliest and almost the smallest nation in Middle Europe.

There, the prince had fallen in love with and married a famous Viennese beauty. Eventually, a few years later, he had fallen in love again, but was still married. There was nothing for it. 'I told my wife I was going on a long expedition and left for the desert. I have been here ever since. I do not believe my wife is unhappy with her present status. For her, I think my most attractive feature was my title.' And he smiled. 'She is fond of sensation. She saw me as an exotic monster and the reality disappointed her. Albinism has been in our family since the Dawn of Time. We carry that stigmata as we carry our motto "Do You The Devil's Work" and defend or pursue the Holy Grail. It is rather easier to follow that motto in the desert . . . Certainly less complicated.' There was a note of self-mockery in his voice.

Poppy said she thought him brave. Such nobility belonged to an earlier, more romantic century. The wild Berberim of these parts were notorious for their savage treatment of strangers. Even she knew that.

He told her that he had never been troubled by the tribes. He had not sought their approval, he said, nor courted them. They understood that he wished to be left to his own devices and seemed to respect that.

'I am not a brave man, Miss Begg. I am a coward, I think. I chose this life because it was the easiest thing I could do. It was a rather selfish choice. I believe it is not uncommon for those of us who seek to escape the emotional complications of the world to become explorers and scientists and such. Believe me, I know that I took the easy way. I have a facility for languages. I was trained to ride and shoot. Nothing I do is very difficult for me. And in my heart I know very well I should have gone back to Mirenburg and faced the consequences – both moral and emotional. Instead, I found a life and a culture which applauded me, respected my love of solitude. My life is not difficult. It's rather simple, in fact, most of the time. With a couple of good camels and enough water, I had no other problems. For years, if I was not happy, at least I was pleasantly distracted. I swear that I did not expect to remain as long as I did. But I found my perfect home and I stayed. I am taking you to that home now. You could be only the third living European to see it.'

He glanced away. She wondered if he expected her to die in the desert. Maybe he planned to kill her? He spoke so openly of his past. Or was he merely willing to trust her own sense of honour? She hoped it was the latter.

They travelled for two more days. She had taken to dozing in her saddle in the afternoons and was only vaguely aware that they pushed farther and farther into the grey-brown semi-desert, what the Far Atlas Berberim called the *rach*, while in the distance lay only the rolling dunes of the unmapped Sahara. It was in the red early evening, with the sun settling in the west, that she opened her eyes to discover they were still on the stony *rach*, but were descending into a shallow valley filling with pink sand, at the end of which were mounds of wind-worn rock. She believed that she deceived herself into catching glimpses of green, but she saw no water.

Poppy Begg knew that she had reached that mysterious corner of the Sahara uncrossed by caravans or tribes but shunned as the home of ifrits and djinns. Ahead lay an horizon without apparent end and, lost in a haze of shimmering silver blue, was the cluster of rocks, looking positively welcoming. 'My home,' said Al Rik'h, pointing. 'They know it as the lost oasis of Kufar'dh. You can see how anyone would believe this area barren.' And he laughed.

As they descended farther down the valley, Poppy began to notice the corroded remains of bones, some of them almost certainly human; of metal tools, weapons, armour, horse furniture and other artefacts – as if all the armies of history had marched here to die.

At last von Bek explained:

'A legend – it was only ever that – concerning the gold of Carthage was always attached to Kufar'dh and brought adventurers here. It still brings one or two. But Kufar'dh has no gold, as far as I know. Though once she must have had it.'

'Only the Grail,' she said, and had the pleasure of seeing the faintest flicker of confusion on his features. Then he laughed, as if she had joked.

'I grew to resent my responsibilities, you know. Perhaps falling in love was a distraction, deliberately engineered? I was, for a while, a gambler. Not at the French tables – at least, not much – but in Mirenburg, for the Game of Time. It was too complex, I suppose. I still remember my duty to the Grail, but I perform it in the old places, the places of that holy cup's genesis, Miss Begg. They say we are the descendants of angels, yet I see no evidence for it, do you?'

His handsome camel reared her head, sniffing and growling. 'She knows we are close to home,' said von Bek. 'You think me a hermit, don't you? Perhaps a little mad? Well, I have a great deal of company here, most of it dead. You see the remains of those who visited here. All the tribes and races of mankind from Zanzibar to Zamarra have come here and will no doubt continue to come while folk tell stories. And will no doubt always be disappointed. I am perhaps the only one not to be. But I did not come looking for the gold of Carthage. I have known this place for twenty years. I have lived here for ten. I found it by accident.'

The rocks rose steeply overhead, taller than they had appeared from a distance, and Poppy could smell water suddenly. Sweet water. She smelled it long before she saw it, protected by a huge tongue of cool limestone hanging over it, a large, clear pool. Foliage, shrubbery, desert flowers, palms were all reflected in the water. But her attention was immediately drawn to the dominant reflection, of glittering blues and geometric yellows and scarlets and dusty browns, and she gasped. She was looking at the tall, ornamental columns of an Egyptian temple! The building was in an astonishing state of preservation. It was like nothing she had seen even at Luxor or Abu Simbal. The temple might have been built that very day.

The vivid hieroglyphs were in the familiar styles, but protected by a clear glaze, evidently of the same period, which here and there had begun to flake. Like the lake that surrounded it, the building was completely invisible either from the air or the surrounding ground. The temple was of local stone. Deep within the rocky overhang, it drew all its light from the water's reflection.

At first only surprised by the state of preservation, Poppy was quick to realise how significant an architectural find this must be. Egypt was three thousand miles away across unrelenting desert! She could not speak for the questions crowding her mind.

Understanding, Ulrich von Bek smiled. 'There's no particular mystery to it, Miss Begg. It is the temple and living quarters of the worshippers of Aton. They believed in a single deity, whom they symbolised by the sun. He bore rather a lot of characteristics in common with our Judaeo-Christian interpretations. This shocking heresy was, they believed, stamped out in Egypt. Clearly it lived on here, with some ups and down, for centuries. Then, little by little, the inhabitants left or died and only their architecture remains of their civilised and disciplined way of life. There is some evidence that the last of them, all ancient, died in defence of their home when the first band of Benin warriors came through.'

Dismounting, they let their animals drink and graze. A wooden bridge stretched from the shore to the little island on which the hidden temple was built. At length, he led her across this. She paused at the first pillar, running slender fingers over the bright paintings. 'All because they disagreed with a religious orthodoxy. They walked three thousand miles until they were sure they were safe. They walked all that way in order to practise their faith!'

'Ironically, they went through a series of apostasies over the centuries. There are records inside. It's clear a pantheon *was* worshipped here, at least for a while. Maybe they invoked the old gods, and the old gods punished them for their desertion of Egypt. Aha!' He paused, his voice becoming gentler. 'Here's a visitor I'm hoping will survive: he was not in a good way when I left!'

On the broad stone apron of the temple, propped against an inner pillar, just outside the huge main door, Poppy saw a young man. He had black hair, dark eyes and an almost feminine mouth. Clearly he was not in his right mind. He gasped and murmured feverishly, unable to focus on them even as they approached.

Prince Ulrich hurried to fetch the boy some water and herbs, which he mixed and presented in a small bowl, doing what he could to make the boy comfortable. He did not seem injured. He wore the uniform of the Spanish Foreign Legion, but with golden eagle wings, showing him to be an air auxiliary. 'A pilot,' she said. 'You found him in the desert?'

'His plane crashed about five miles away.' Von Bek had seen it go down.

'Is she here?' said the boy suddenly in Spanish. 'Is she here?'

Prince von Bek tried to calm him, but the young pilot would have none of it. He clawed at the albino's burnoose and veil. 'You must tell me the truth. Believe me, I'm strong. It is the wondering which is weakening me. Please, my dear fellow, tell me the truth!'

Prince von Bek nodded. He knew that he owed the boy that degree. of respect. 'She is not alive,' he said.

'Oh, my God!' The boy almost shrieked his horror. Yet the herbs had restored him. He turned away, then spoke. 'You got to the place. It was the right place? She was there? You were too late.' Another, long pause, then: 'How did she die?'

Von Bek's compassion took hold of him.

'By her own hand,' he said, and rose to his feet.

He and Poppy Begg walked to the far end of the apron, staring into the perfect waters of the oasis, listening, with as much self-control as they could muster, to the boy's appalling weeping.

A little later, when the boy slept, von Bek lit an enormous Byzantine candelabra and by its guttering flames displayed the interior of the temple, the massive public rooms decorated with images of Ra and the Aton, before which bowed, in homage, the old beast-headed gods of Egypt – the cow, the panther, the goat, the ram and the jackal, the hawk and the lion. This strange pantheon, depicted as all-powerful in so many Egyptian paintings, were here the subjects of Aton. In the smaller chambers other stories were told, other beliefs depicted. He showed her the chambers of the priests and their families, their kitchens, their meetings rooms, their sarcophagi. In the kitchen, using methods older than time, he made her a delicious couscous, which she ate with considerable relish, enthusing on his virtues until he was driven to go and see how the Spanish boy was doing.

'He's weak,' reported von Bek. Making sure that she had eaten and drunk all she needed, he led her to a small, comfortably furnished chamber which appeared to have something of a woman's touch to it, with brocaded shawls and richly woven carpets festooned over an ottoman and a massive brass bed. He was pleased by her surprise. 'I have had time to come by most of the comforts of Europe,' he said. 'This is your room. It was originally intended for a mourning chamber or a tomb. You may use my home in any way you please.

All that I ask is that you remain with the boy if I am gone for any reason.' He hesitated, then said: 'I had occasion to take his service revolver. You will find it behind the main altar in the central temple. It has four rounds. I cannot see that you will need it, but it is as well to know.'

Before she could question him further, the albino had disappeared back into the passages and chambers of his strange, adopted home.

Before she went to sleep, she explored the room, smoking one of the slim, brown cigarettes he had given her, a local kind. Soon she became drowsy and a sense of extraordinary well-being filled her, in spite of the image of the weeping boy still occupying her thoughts. With a sigh, she prepared for rest, changing into the old-fashioned white cotton and lace nightgown provided for her, then climbed into the high bed, to sink into a feather mattress and huge, down pillows. She barely had time to reflect on the peculiar paradox of such luxury, in the middle of a region known as the Forbidden Desert, before she fell into a profound sleep.

Anubis was the first to visit her. The jackal-headed god, wise and compassionate, was dressed in a suit of dark silk, his linen brilliant, almost incandescent. He held a deck of cards in his slender hands and offered to teach her to play. *I will teach you to play with the gods themselves*, he said. *I am your master. I am your friend.* And he grew to twice his original size, until his head touched the dark ceiling of her chamber and he glared down at her and he smiled. *Lord Anubis*, he said, and the words were a growl of deep satisfaction with his condition and his power. *Lord Anubis*.

I have no words, she said, *for addressing a god. Nor for parleying with the dead. I am not of your people.*

I will make you mine. It takes nothing for that. I promise. I shall neither smite nor devour thee. Sweet slave. I am your kind master. You have no power save that which I bestow upon thee.

But after Anubis came Set and Horus and Osiris, with the heads of snakes and birds and mammals, and all had the stink of the beast, the fetid stench of animal power, the terrible stench of inevitable death. And she recoiled and she wept and begged for their mercy and they granted it, they said. All she had to do was accept their rule, their arrogant existence, and she would live without pain. Then came Aton, striding into the already crowded room, his face a blinding ball of fire, his voice the rich roll of thunder, his hands ablaze with lightnings, his body boiling with a strange, multi-coloured dust. Aton-Ra the all-powerful, all-seeing. Aton-Ra, tasting the boyhood of a jubilant monotheism, conscious that he somehow carried with him a power greater than all these combined, yet still a barbarian god, still bearing the unmistakable hint of the beast.

She expected him to save her. To dismiss these others. But instead he smiled upon them all as a master might smile upon his favourite pets at play and he vanished. It occurred to her that, as yet, he was unwilling or afraid to test his strength.

Anubis took her up. His eyes were without malice and his white fangs gleamed in a grin of kindness. And they flew across all the magnificent cities of the world, in all their ages and conditions, and then she returned. She lay in her bed watching as the races and nations of mankind marched across the room.

And then they were gone and there was a silence.

She became aware of movement, in corners, beneath furniture, inside draperies and against walls. Small, flickering movements at first, and tiny sounds, almost laughter, perhaps weeping. She strained to hear and then, as the sounds grew louder, tried to block them, gasping and shouting against the insinuating horror of the greedy dead. Out of the walls and the quilts and the pillows they came; out of the carpets and the brocades, the cupboards and the chests, barely seen at first. The greedy dead. All those restless ghouls who had sought gold at the Temple of Aton and had found only painful, prolonged death. Now it was not gold they yearned for, but a little warm blood, a taste of human life, of living flesh and a vibrant soul. They were so hungry, they said. We are forbidden the Afterlife.

She felt the weight of the wraiths upon her body. She sensed that they sought some means of sucking the lifestuff from her. To keep themselves alive – if this were life – for a few more pointless years.

Then she grew even more terrified. What if it were only she? What if it were some specific chemistry of her own that attracted these phantoms?

She began to scream. But door upon door had been closed, all the way to the far exterior, and nothing could hear her, unless it wanted to.

And then Anubis had returned, dismissing the wraiths with familiar contempt, his muzzle curling back over his teeth in a grin of disgust. Within seconds they were all gone. He knelt beside her bed and took her hand. His snout was soft against her skin, his breath warm and moist. *This is our final tomb. So little sustains us now. I am the beast and the beast is your enemy. But it is you I would have live.*

The boy, she said. *The boy is weak. He has no will to live. He has no belief left. Help him with the strength he needs.*

[164]

I will go to him soon and I promise you I will guide him safely into the Land of Death, for this tomb is the gateway to that land.

No, she said. *It is life which must be asserted now. Help him, I beg you. You bring us death. I offer you life.*

There is more than you know, said Anubis. *For every death there is new life. For every tomb a cradle.* He gestured and she stared into the blackness of the ether, into the blossoming stars, into the broad rays of multi-coloured light which radiated everywhere and made paths. Down these moonbeam roads strode all the old gods of Egypt, the beast-headed immortals of Assyria and Babylon, and of Carthage. To stand before her, as if in gratitude. She lowered her eyes against their alien brilliance, averted her head from their heavy stink, and for a moment they regarded her gravely before seeming to make a decision amongst themselves. There was a chorus of shrieks and bellowings: their language. When she looked back, the moonbeams were fading and she saw the last of the old gods disappearing into the great, rich darkness of the ether; and soon there were only stars. Then she saw only the walls of the tomb, her chamber, and she was again alone.

Anubis was gone. Anubis, and with him all the rest of the pantheon. She closed her eyes tight against any further visions and slept dreamlessly until morning.

When she found the Spanish boy, he was much stronger. He spoke of having seen a jackal come to the pool and drink in the moonlight. The jackal had remained, sitting and watching him, all night. Only at dawn had the creature risen and loped off into the desert. The boy believed that the jackal carried the spirit of his dead girl. 'She lives in the desert now, where she was always happiest, where she was free.

'That is my consolation.' She went to find Al Rik'h, but his camel was gone. The boy reported that the albino had left early, riding off in the same direction as the jackal.

'He went into the lands of the Beni Rabi'. He told me he had a duty to perform. I am familiar with those warlike Taureqs. They allow none but their own blood kin to ride with them, yet he is welcome among them.'

Von Bek had not told the young airman when he would return.

Poppy Begg was still lost in the memory of her vivid dreams. She had never experienced such complex illusions. She could even recall the smell of those creatures: that stink of ancient vitality. She remembered the kindness of Anubis and she knew that he had answered her prayer. He had brought some comfort, at least, to the Spanish airman.

She wondered for a moment if Prince Ulrich von Bek had deliberately exposed her to whatever old magic still soaked the stones of the tomb he had turned into a bedchamber. One day she would ask him.

Meanwhile, she thought often of the jackal. When she returned to her bed that night, he came to her again.

To claim, he reminded her gently, his price.

How Vengeance Came To Th'amouent

Poppy Begg busied herself all that week tending to the young airman and watching him grow stronger and sadder by the hour. Her clear, grey eyes were full of sympathy for him. At length he asked her if he might tell her his story. She had been too discreet to propose it. She said that he must not weaken himself. She would let him talk, but if he grew too tired, she would stop him. He was like a child now, almost wholly obedient to her tender will.

He told her at once who the young woman had been.

'She was my wife,' he said. 'I had not seen her for three years.' He had met her in Casablanca and they had fallen in love. Against the wishes of her father and his own parents, they had married. Life in the army had been difficult. He took an extended leave and they went to live in Madrid, then in Paris.

Poppy suggested there had been problems involving race, but the young lieutenant shook his head. 'She was Caucasian, with that clear, pale skin and aquiline beauty of the Western Berber. She looked, to European eyes, every inch an aristocrat of an old family. Most people assumed her to be Viennese. Our problems had to do with her restlessness. I should have taken her away from the desert. Like you, she sought exotic romance, but unlike you she did not live to learn a lesson. She disappeared one night, near Les Halles. I became frantic and began searching for her. I searched for a year without success, without a single clue, and eventually I was forced to rejoin my regiment. I prayed that I might find her back in the Magrib. Here, at least, there were rumours, a fragment of hope.'

'You heard of her?'

'She heard of me. She learned that I was stationed in Tangier and she got word to me. She had been sold to the Caliph of Th'amouent and was a prisoner in his cruel household. She begged me to help her escape. There were people to bribe, others to cajole or to blackmail, and so on. It took me six months. I raised all the money I could, paid whoever might require a bribe, and I was successful. My wife was freed with the help of a high-ranking servant of the Caliph. She was given a map, a compass and a horse. She was also given instructions for reaching the Wadi-al-Hara, the River of Stones. There, I might safely land my aeroplane. The rest is everything you might have guessed. My plane crashed here. I had engine trouble. I was tormented with the vision of my wife waiting alone by the Wadi-al-Hara, expecting me at any moment – and so vulnerable, so horribly vulnerable, to the Caliph's forces, who would track her as a matter of principle as soon as it was discovered that she was gone. She had already let me know the fate of any woman who sought to escape his harem. If they caught her, they would be allowed to determine how she would be punished, whether to finish her by stoning or flaying, and what to do with her in the meantime. Then, because the Caliph is a cautious man, anxious not to upset the sensibilities of his foreign investors, they would dismember and butcher the corpse beyond recognition . . .'

At this the young Spaniard broke down. He rapidly took control of himself, but could not speak for a while.

Later Poppy learned how Al Rik'h had found the young man in the wrecked plane. He was already feverish, babbling of his wife's danger and pleading with the crimson-eyed aristocrat to take him to her, to save her. Instead the Secret One had made him comfortable and had gone rapidly in search of the woman.

Poppy assumed that this was all he knew of the story, but now he revealed that Al Rik'h had spoken long into the night. According to the albino, his wife had stabbed herself when she saw the Caliph's men riding down on her and no sign of the aeroplane, but was still alive when they reached her. It was then that Al Rik'h had arrived at the Wadi-al-Har and disposed rapidly of the ruffians before they could touch the woman. She was still alive when he had dealt with the Caliph's riders, but only barely. She had whispered her desperate request into her saviour's ear – that he tell her father, Sheikh Aron ben Sid', that she loved him and had never meant to shame him and to tell her husband that she had never willingly betrayed him.

'And where has he gone now?' Poppy's lovely face was full of pity and concern. She brushed her brown hair back from her cheeks and turned her head away, so that he might not see the tears. She was not puzzled by the discrepancy in the story. Clearly Al Rik'h had wanted to spare the young flyer's feelings.

[167]

'I think he intends to deliver the other part of her message,' said the lieutenant. 'He has gone out there' – he indicated the depths of the far Sahara – 'to seek Sheikh Aron, who is the great patriarch of the Beni Rabi' and counts Le Loup Blanc as his son. Von Bek will be welcome. My wife, you see, was Sheikh Aron's daughter. I think that for once the Caliph of Th'amouent has misjudged his enemy.'

Together they prepared to wait for the return of the Secret One. On some nights, Poppy Begg did not visit her chamber, but tended to the young airman, cradling his head on her breast as he slept and murmured and wept in his dreams.

They were not to see Al Rik'h again for another five days, when he brought them fresh horses and provisions and instructed them on how they might reach Th'amouent. He seemed distant and thoughtful and would tell them nothing of what had taken place between himself and the Ben Rabi'.

'I think you will swiftly come to know the end of this particular tale,' he assured them.

When they arrived at last in Th'amouent, Poppy found the character of the city subtly changed. She was thankful that her uncle had waited for her. He already knew that she was safe.

'There is a new master of the city,' he told her. 'A new Caliph. Th'amouent has only just finished celebrating the end of tyranny.'

He had seen the whole affair from his rooms, he said, when one morning, without warning, the veiled warriors of the Ben Rabi' had ridden their magnificent horses and camels through the Hakhim Gate and streamed through Th'mouent's narrow streets to surround the palace of the Caliph, their blue cloaks rising and falling in the wind like a vengeful tide. Then, at a word from their white-faced leader, they had engulfed the palace. And by evening the city was informed that the Caliph, his kin and all his favourite servants were dead or in the process of dying and that Th'amouent was now under the protection of Allah and his faithful servant the Sheikh Aron ben Sid' of the Beni Rabi'. The flayed corpses were displayed in the D'Jemaa-al-Jehudim; the glaring heads preserved in salt. It was what the populace expected and demanded of their new Caliph.

But Poppy Begg remained all the more in love with the crimson-eyed albino, who had returned to his forbidden desert, to his strange, god-haunted home.

Poppy Begg stayed for many months in Th'amouent and was treated with extravagant and courteous hospitality by the new Caliph, who readily assumed his responsibilities and seemed willing to treat her as the daughter he had lost. But Al Rik'h, his Zulu companion Lobangu and their snow-white camels were reported as having been seen in the mountains of Abyssinia, helping the people against the Italian invaders.

Poppy yearned for the aristocratic albino and prayed for him to come to her. Though she asked after him often, she kept her word to him. She never told of the lost oasis, of the hidden temple or of the visions she had experienced there. She showed a certain interest in images of Anubis, and read much of Egyptian antiquity. And she did not offer the Spanish airman the true story he would never hear, once he was gone from the region, of his wife's death.

The Spaniard was ordered one day to Marrakech, to take the army train to Tangier. There was news of an uprising amongst the Rif, of a charismatic leader who threatened to drive all Christians into the sea and seemed able to keep his word. The young airman would die in an early expedition against Abd'-al-Krim, brought down by the long guns of the Berber sharpshooters.

At last Sir Albert Begg came out to find her. It was early 1939 and the volatile politics of Europe had drawn attention away from expansionist dreams in Africa, at least for the moment.

Sir Albert persuaded his niece to return with him to England. He could not otherwise vouch for her safety. Soon the power of the British Empire would be stretched to the full and there would be parts of the world where it would not stretch at all . . .

Until the Blitz of 1940, in which she acquitted herself with some heroism, Poppy Begg was more bored in London than ever before, dreaming each night of an Egyptian temple, preserved almost as new, hidden in a lost oasis, deep within the forbidden Sahara. She dreamed, too, of a white rider on a white camel, a rider whose deep-set crimson eyes looked with affection into hers and whose kiss drew the soul from her body. She dreamed of Anubis the Jackal God, who would come to make love to her, to carry her away into the depths of the ancient Sahara, where all our histories were written in the dust which blew perpetually across the dunes in that deep, unmapped wilderness that is the world beyond the West. She dreamed of prehistoric lusts, of supernatural satisfactions, of the great, bestial intelligences whose law still threatened the living. She dreamed, again and again, everything she had dreamed before, in that hidden temple, where time and even entropy were forgotten. And all the while the bombs fell around her and her city blazed.

One day, after the end of the Second World War, but just before the Egyptian Revolution, which ejected Farouk and the British, she went to live in Egypt, a famous recluse. She has a homestead of sorts there still, above Aswan, looking down upon the great white rocks of the first and second cataracts, still busy with the traffic of centuries.

They say she worships the old gods, that she is a witch, but a benign one. She is almost a mascot to the local people. There was never any trouble here, up on the Nubian border. Not the sort they had in Cairo. They say she goes into the deepest desert, where the ancients built a tomb for Aton, their dead god, and that at night the old pantheon visits her, disporting with her and telling her all the secrets of Time.

Sometimes, in the afternoons, she will lay out her tea service and entertain her friend, the Wesleyan chaplain of the Cataract Hotel favoured chiefly these days by German tourists of the old school. He rarely removes his dark glasses. He has the face of a Jesuit and some believe him miraculously recovered from leprosy. He is in fact a pure albino, of uncertain age.

The old couple are enjoying their last years. They sit in Miss Begg's wicker chairs, below the slow, lazy fans, and tell stories, one after another, until the sun goes down over the Nile.

And, perhaps occasionally, on a warm, spring evening, the chaplain will inquire politely if it would be convenient for him to stay the night.

And, politely, she will assure him of his welcome.

Poppy Begg was prompted next to tell a blood-curdling tale she'd heard in the Orient, about a man given the choice of losing his testicles or pulling his own eye out of his head. At the end of it, the company made excuses and began to leave. Poppy chose to walk in the gardens for half-an-hour or so while Jack Karaquazian found Squire Begg's PC and idly tapped out a message on the keys . . .

10. *the enigma windows*

CHAPTER ONE

Mouse User's Guide

'From now on, these are the questions you'll be asking before you buy software.'

Microsoft, 1994

Jerry Cornelius wasn't feeling well. He hated having his sleep interrupted in the middle of a decade. He checked his watches, It was either 1995 or 2005. He sighed, threw his towel on his coffin and climbed back into his old street duds. As he clicked on the remote the Bland Assassins were doing *Don't Ask, Don't Look* on a Golden Oldies show. He had picked a very bad option. He hated anniversaries. This was going to be a rotten 1995.

It was surprising how much you missed your mum.

Some mornings he wished he'd never been downloaded.

CHAPTER TWO

Turning Off Your System

'No one makes it easier to do what you really want.'

IBM, 1994

Overhead, a badly printed sign warned that he was entering a low air quality neighbourhood. Automatically he slipped his gasmask down to cover his mouth and drove steadily into the sepia haze. Even with

[171]

his mask on he could not ignore the smell of smouldering garbage, the main source of energy in this designated Green Zone.

As he turned right into Blenheim Crescent he peered through the smog at the family flat, but the whole house was now a burned out shell. Smoke still curled from the basement where his mother had spent her last years and was probably the chief source of the stench.

Sometimes he longed for his mother to be restored. It had been the end of the family when she died. Was this obsession with finding his sister and brother in any sense rational?

He took a left into Portobello Road, where black market air merchants sold recycled Australian ozone and the popular blend known as 'Lapland Blue', a fairly noxious mix of Siberian Second Filter and various odourless fumes from the innovative Swedish factories of the Arctic Circle, originally issued as emergency rations to Russian nationals. The Swedes were still investigating the viability of making cheap artificial air, or *Volksluft* as the Greens were fond of calling it.

Through the mass of teenage pimps and middle class whores Jerry drove with gentle insistence, avoiding eye contact for fear he would be recognised by his more obscure relatives.

He paid a couple of personable gang boys to keep his Duesenberg safe and entered the dodgy airlock of *The Begging Novelist*, known in better days as *The Old Boar*, one of his mother's favourites of the 1950s. He wished there were some way of bringing her back.

He didn't remove his mask. The cigarillo smoke was thicker than the atmosphere outside.

At the bar he ordered himself a large Vortex Water from Peewee Wilson, the sour landlord, and turned to observe his fellow customers. They were a sorry crew of ancient bohemians, petty crooks and con-artists on hard times, talking of better days, when it had been their world and run on decent liberal lines. The bar vibrated with the brisk whine of disappointed class expectations. In the old Ladies' Snug, now without its door, Billy 'the Bishop' Beesley, his pale lips rimmed with cheap chocolate, his many chins shaking with indignation, deplored the decline in moral values.

'I was all for air privatisation from the beginning. We have to pay the proper price for everything we consume. It's the only way of regulating the law. You have to balance your books, don't you? They thought they could go on recycling a few cans forever. Now listen to them yelping when they can't afford their gas and electricity and have to start carrying coals for those old Victorian fireplaces in earnest. There's a rare treat.'

He cast lascivious eyes on the Mars bar gripped in the hand of his wicked daughter Mitzi, who licked it slowly, as if to challenge him. It was unusual for them both to be out of jail at the same time and they were celebrating this happy coincidence. The trade wasn't what it had been in their Golden Age, which had ended so tragically with poor Maggie's betrayal and the crushing of her cause.

'Air privatisation was strictly green. People'have to learn to value God's commodities. You know that and I know that, Flash, old man.' He addressed his raincoated companion who stared with sleazy abstraction upon Mitzi's trim figure and fingered his buttons nostalgically. 'But try telling these whinging liberals what really put their property values down and they'd lynch you if they weren't so bloody feeble. What could Maggie do when she did come back? Six months and she was forced to leave for Majorca to restore her health. She couldn't have done anything else. Too much damage had been wreaked, old boy.

'That's very good of you. I'll take a pint of Ackroyd's if it's filtered.

'Personally,' Billy continued, 'I don't miss the telly. How much electricity did our grandfathers need?'

'I mourn the Age of Steam.' Mitzi climbed onto a bar stool and smoothed her skirt over her thighs. Then she shifted her holstered Browning to a more comfortable position. 'Remember, pa?'

'I remember when it was all microchips and mobile phones round here. Cable. Everything.' Flash Gordon's eyes glazed with horrible nostalgia and he brushed compulsively at his greasy mackintosh. He had been a successful ticket scalper in the years when anyone could come and go in the West End at will without an expensive zoning permit. Ironically, he had never been able to get a foothold in the permit trade.

The Bishop looked round suddenly and stared full into Jerry's eyes. The shock made Jerry feel sick.

Then Beesley had turned away and murmured something to Mitzi who became immediately alert. Jerry could almost hear her panting. It was time to leave. It had been foolish of him to expect to find anything worthwhile of his past here. He pushed through a crowd of petitioners and mendicants, all with their own particular tale of woe, and settled his gasmask over his face until all he could hear was the sound of his own breath. He wondered how much it was worth these days.

He had hoped for news, at least, of his sister Catherine and his estate agent brother Frank. He could not believe they would leave

London. But there was a good chance that they too were dead. Or at least well-hidden.

Hot tears sprang suddenly from his romantic eyes. For a short while, as he reached the street, he was blind. Then his mask cleared and he saw he had returned to his car just in time. His fee was about to run out. Already the gang boys were fingering their spray cans and casting artistic eyes over the Duesenberg's antique gloss.

CHAPTER THREE

Cleaning Your Mouse

'It's not about the highway, it's about you.'
AT&T, 1994

It was a relief to breathe the sweetened air of Mayfair. There was something to be said for a secured environment, at least for a holiday. Jerry showed his pass to his old sidekick Shakey Mo Beck who had changed his name and now worked here as a guard. 'Good job I know you, Mr C,' he said. 'We don't let just any old scum in here, no matter what papers they got. We had that Edward Heath round last week, saying he'd left his stereo in his old flat. He'd have to try harder than that, I told him. They're all the same these days, aren't they, sir? I say to them — 'course you can pinch yourself a computer or buy one for fifty quid, but what you going to use for power when you got all that fancy stuff? I say. Good luck, sir.'

Jerry shuddered as Mo saluted. Mo had always been fond of uniforms and regulations and Mayfair answered his deepest yearnings. Mo was profoundly gratified by the new world order.

Heavy feet bore Jerry deep into the luxuried West.

Strolling through Grosvenor Square, filled with the heady murmuring of smooth-running electronics, Jerry was more relaxed than anyone around him. There was something he was doing or some way he was looking which made them nervous. He had an impression of agitated bleating. No doubt he carried the smell of the Green Zones on him, the perfume of ecological sacrifice, the smack of some undesired reality. (Here, it was chic to wear a VR helmet in the shape of a gasmask when playing 'Street' and its generics.) Their notion of the outside was an exciting mix of sex, violence, and sudden death, rather than the dreary round of fuel- and food-gathering which was daily reality in the Green Zones. The zoners weren't much of a Mob at all, really.

He was entranced by the glamorous window displays. He had better get some new clothes while he was here.

Skirting the Cadogan Mall's cobbled elegance, its fantasy of copper oaks and steel birches, Jerry entered the Old Bond Street Tube, now a business facility offering several hundred preconnected stations. He clicked on the unit menu and found Miss Brunner at the third level, an unfashionable location. The thought of seeing her again didn't do his stomach any good, but she was one of the few survivors of the information wars who might be able to help him. He felt driven to open all possible options.

As he took the elevator down, a sharp voice warned him that any accident which might occur in the complex would be regarded as his responsibility. He was advised by purring feminine tones that he could buy quick and reliable cover at the screen on his left. The screen accepted all major cards.

In an endless spiral of cubicles he found her working on a shabby old laptop which must have been almost two years old. She had made some attempt to disguise its age with decals and polish, but there was no mistaking the obsolete toolbars and the crude palette. She might also have retrieved it from a recyke or one of those charities which specialised in trying to wire up the poor who, notoriously, were given to spending any power units they received on games and home entertainment, rather than self-improvement, which was why the sale of batteries was now controlled and 'piles noires' changed hands at crack-high prices. He remembered the sixties, when they had both worked on the huge cryogenic Leos and mechanically-driven IBMs which filled whole buildings, when she had been the world's top programmer.

But her skills had been devoted to insane, formulaic politics and complex delusions. She had been on the verge of making a self-reproducing, omniscient hermaphrodite, which she had conceived as the beginning of a new stage in human evolution, containing the sum of all our experience. But in the end her conventional training and social ambitions had sidetracked into the 80s experiments, when everyone was trying to produce the perfect prole consumer. This led her into the series of cheap scams and grandiose investment portfolios which had ruined her. The information revolution had come without her.

By the time Westminster had got her first environment-control station and gone over to a single chip structure which, once the bugs were out of it, made it possible to dispense with all human units, Miss Brunner was exited. She had little real hope of ever getting back into the system. But she clung on somehow, flooding the world's mail-boxes with her oracular warnings. Her screen, before she closed it, was lively with phrases like 'tougher measures', 'strong medicine' and 'old-fashioned values', just one more exhausted political vocabulary. Nowadays the common sensibility was expressed by the rhetoric of the Greens which used terms like 'good husbandry' and 'environmental responsibility' to advertise their virtue.

Miss Brunner's red hair was streaked with black and grey and her eyes were wild when, muttering, she finally looked up and recognised him. 'Belphegor!'

For a moment she was terrified, then she said calmly: 'You should do something about those spots.' But there was no real venom in her voice. She was worn out. She turned her eyes back and was reabsorbed in her screen.

'I was looking for Catherine and Frank,' said Jerry. 'Have they left town, do you know?'

Her thin fingers automatically sought the answer. She mumbled to herself as she surfed her options. 'Yes. There they are. Both of them.' She grew calculating. 'What do you want to know for? What's it worth?'

Carelessly, Jerry put a stack of energy cards on her console, enough to keep her in Mayfair for another year at least.

'You little wanker,' she said. 'What have you sold?'

CHAPTER FOUR

Memory Configuration

'With 90 MHz, we're the power source as well as
the energy source.'

Acer, 1994

In desperation Jerry tried again to get Jimi Hendrix to work, but it was no good. Clearly, Jimi had been digitally blanded for maximum marketing and was playing at a subtly slower speed. Jerry had very few escape routes left. Every path he took seemed to wind up in a blank screen.

Back in Ladbroke Grove he waited while a slow moving recycling convoy, of carts and old prams, crossed at Elgin Crescent. On the pavement the children had chalked crude access ikons, as if this simple magic would bring them the electronic benefits they craved. Their rags were crimson and royal blue, vivid greens and yellows, saturated with the power dyes once fashionable in the secured environments until it was discovered that they caused infertility. Now the thrift shops of Notting Dale and Hammersmith were full of them. Rumour was that only such dyed clothing was now distributed to the poor.

There was a popular notion in the secured environments that teen-agers got deliberately pregnant in order to sell the babies for cash. The V channels had been full of the story for almost a day, forcing the government to declare War on Brood Mares, demand the ritual resignation of a junior minister and promise to rid the country of this new vice by the end of the week. The scandal had been revived later as a Slum Doctor story ('Medics Who Break The Rules', *The London & TV Times*) concerning those practitioners disbarred for illegal fee-cutting. Sometimes the outlaw doctors even worked for nothing. They threatened the entire stability of society and the efficiency of the healthcare industry.

It seemed that Frank had some connection with illegal treatments of non-citizens. Once again he was bringing shame on the family name. Shareholders were dumping health stock in wads as the word got around about its sluggish improvement in contrast to diagnostic electronics. Doctors who refused to pull their economic weight were doing nobody any good in the long run. It was admittedly hard to imagine Frank giving something for nothing. Perhaps he was more in the pharmaceutical side of the business, where he had most experience.

Jerry checked the address on his screen. An arrow pointed to Tavistock Mews and the repair shop which had been there since he was a boy. Frank had seriously gone to ground.

Parking the Duesenberg where he could see it, Jerry made his way through the discarded engines and methane converters, the shells of useless limos and compacts, the debris of a more optimistic age. There wasn't much work for a car mechanic in this part of the world. The place had to be a front – a crackhouse or some sort of backroom ozone outfit. An oily Yorkshire terrier yawned at him as he crossed the threshold of the shop and gingerly entered the gloom. There was someone working in a shaft of light from a transom window high in the roof. When they heard him, they tried to hide

[177]

what they were doing, but Jerry knew an illegal accumulator when he saw one.

'Take it easy, Frank,' said Jerry. 'It's only me.'

'*Only you! Only you!*' Frank was already hysterical. His voice had nowhere to go but down. 'I thought you'd crashed!'

'Just for a season, Frank. Believe me, I'm not used to these hours.'

'You shouldn't be here. You're fiction now. A myth. Hadn't you heard?'

'That's always happening. It's not hard to stop it. I've gone for a sharper image. Where's Catherine, Frank? You haven't done anything nasty, have you? You know how impressionable she is.'

'Don't VR me, Jerry. I'm hip to that.' He spoke uncertainly, peering carefully up into his brother's glowing face. Then he touched Jerry's hand. It burned like Lunar ice and left scarlet skin. 'I've been cold,' he said. 'It's a chill. Don't pull away like that. You're my brother.'

'Where's Catherine? Is there anything left?'

'I've been cold, Jerry. I'm not well. It's what she would have wanted. You know what a brick she was. She'd do anything for you, Jerry. More than she would for me, even. But she's done a lot for me, I'm not complaining.'

'Where have you got her you slimy little bastard? How many times must we run this option, Frank? What's happened to our history? Are we doomed to an infinity of recycling?'

'I presume these are all rhetorical questions.' Frank put his keyboard under his arm and reached for the handle of his portable. 'I'll have to be exiting now.'

Jerry pulled his needle-gun from its holster and blew the dust off its barrel. 'It wouldn't be the first time I shot you.'

'It wouldn't be the first time you'd bloody killed me, but that doesn't get either of us anywhere we want to go. The ikons are all changed, Jerry. And the bloke who knows the key gets the power, right? You know what I'm saying? I got the power. I got the power.' Even as Jerry watched, Frank's image wiped into negative and then ran through a series of gender options as if, by imitating Jerry's earlier experience, he would become Jerry. Working on some sort of ramshackle transference programme, he hadn't reckoned on Jerry's homecoming. Jerry forgot his needle-gun and dived for the bench. He had seen the remote. Frank screamed.

Too late. Within an instant Frank had been refiled.

Without remorse, Jerry slipped the diskette into the pocket of his black car coat. 'What's the time? My watch has stopped.' For a moment he was surprised when his brother didn't answer. No doubt he would have to learn a whole new series of commands.

CHAPTER FIVE

Magnum User's Guide

'Excite your senses.'
Quantex, 1994

Gently Jerry pulled the filebox from the stack and looked down at the pale, frozen face of his beautiful sister. She was thin and gaunt. It had taken him four days at the keyboard to find her. Frank had hidden her well before exhausting her of all but a fraction of her energy. Just enough to keep her ticking over. Jerry wasn't sure how he was going to retrieve her. If necessary he would have to call in Miss Brunner with her spells and blood-sacrifices, but he thought he had the skills to bring her back. There was not much time. If necessary, he thought, his sister could be restored to him by the power of his will alone.

Swiftly he surfed every possible option, following every path that presented itself. He hit transfusion mode and found a way of getting some blood into her. Now her ivory skin was tinged with rose. But still her breathing was insubstantial and there was no detectable pulse.

He plunged on, following the most unlikely clues, running simultaneous French, English, Russian, Chinese and Arabic searches on different frames. It was only an hour or so until sunset and he knew instinctively he would lose her forever if he failed to revive her before daybreak. His hands were frantic at his board. The light of the flashing screen was the livid light of Hell, reflected in his blood-red eyes, on his bone-white skin and the gleaming velvet of his black car coat.

His energy was low and he was growing reconciled to oblivion when he found the cauldron ikon and clicked to the grimoire. The ingredients could only be found by one route in that time frame. He went to VR and scrambled through scenario after scenario to gather everything he needed.

Twenty minutes later he threw in his last mouse and began the bastardised Latin Miss Brunner usually employed for the spell.

'*Ab ovo usque ad mala! Corporate, corporatumi. Ad majorem, Asmoday gloriam. Da locum melioribus.*'

THANK YOU, said his screen, THIS SPELL HAS BEEN BROUGHT TO YOU COURTESY OF ALCHEMICAL SYSTEMS OF HOUSTON, SERVING ALL YOUR NECROMANTIC NEEDS.

Jerry decided to get through this as quickly as possible. He had no clear idea of the meaning of the words which poured from his mouth, but clearly it was doing the trick. He bellowed with triumph, skin blazing copper, eyes blazing emerald, as he saw his sister rise in an aura of silver and reach vibrant arms towards him, everything Frank had stolen from her restored.

He gathered her to him, holding her tightly as his equipment bucked and throbbed, blowing suddenly in a haze of dissipating power. But she was safe.

He carried her over the floor littered with fused cables and melted casings, out across the hissing metal and blackened circuits, through the lifting darkness of the dawn to the two million dollar environmentally controlled BMWMG-R which would bear them to Paradise. There was no point in worrying about the people you left behind. As long as you looked after your immediate family, there wasn't much more you could do. A new, primitive spirit was abroad. Life was simpler now that it was fully privatised and the Law maintained by the tribal feud or the payment of blood-money. Society was rapidly being deconstructed. The future belonged to the highest bidder.

Jerry had what he had come for. It was time to get on his bike and head for some happier century. There was a price to be paid for time travel, but it was worth it sometimes just to confront the devil you knew. All his futures had been abolished. Everything ahead was uncertain and no doubt dangerous, the threat of many kinds of death. The triumph of entropy. The end of consciousness. It was impossible to plot a course.

For the moment, at least, he could hope for nothing but a few hours with his sister in some impossible sanctuary.

He settled her in the passenger seat and started the command procedures. He heard the car's filters growling softly as they accepted the smog. He lounged back from his controls, clicked on GO, and let nature take her course.

By the time Jack Karaquazian returned to the flat, Colinda was already in bed. She was reading, the light of the small screen harsh on her perfect features. She kissed him absently as he climbed in. He sighed and relaxed.

'You're looking better, Jack,' she told him.

He smiled. 'I'm feeling it,' he said.

11. *epilogue the birds of the moon*

'The established migratory patterns of
certain species of birds are now well
understood. While some birds fly
South in the Winter or North in the
Summer, others migrate regularly to
the Moon where, at the warm heart
of our Satellite, they feed off a rich
diet of moon-worms and other grubs.
The great under-ground Gardens of
the Moon, developed from the natural
character of the Asteroid by generations
of settlers, are a source of wonder to all
travellers privileged to visit them.'

> James Audubon,
> *The Birds of the Moon,*
> New Orleans, 1926.

CHAPTER ONE

Avoiding Diversions

Tommy Beck pulled the Tranny over to the side of the road and
brought it to a careful stop with the engine running. He needed some
sleep. Against the grey horizon and the rising sun, a milk float and a
breakdown lorry had looked like a police blockade. He folded back

his map and checked his route. He needed to start turning west just after Witney, following the invisible lines as best he could, taking the roads they most closely paralleled. He hoped this time he would get where he wanted to go. Every summer for twenty-three years he had retraced their journey back and forth across the country, trying to match exactly the meandering route he and Joany and the kids had taken for Glastonbury and the first festival.

Even his friends weren't too sure of Tommy's sanity. People thought Joany had run off. Someone had even said he'd abused his children.

Tommy knew what had really happened. He ignored the scepticism, the antagonism, the zealots who wanted to use his experience for themselves. He kept his own counsel and his own course.

Since that first Glastonbury, Tommy Beck had attempted to reproduce their original route. He spent much of his spare time reading and studying for it. Every year he arrived at Glastonbury Tor and climbed to where caution had betrayed him, where he had seen the air, stinking of roses and vanilla, seal itself over an impossible view, separating him from his wife and children, dooming him to all these years of self-disgust and obsession. He knew what had happened, even if he no longer spoke of it to anyone. He had last seen Joany and the kids standing on that broad band of road, like a wide shaft of moonlight, arcing into the richly coloured darkness of the ether: he had the impression of great caravans of people and animals flowing back and forth, as if every creature that had ever existed was still alive.

Tommy Beck had always been of a practical disposition, valuable to the communes he joined. He smoked a modest amount of dope and did the odd tab of acid only if it was really good. He was widely read and could repair any small engine ever made. His attraction to Glastonbury had been entirely social. He had never been prepared for what had happened twenty-four years ago.

In their old Commer van, full of friends, looking foward to listening to some music and having a good time in the sun, they left their Notting Dale squat and headed west. It felt wonderful, as if the millennium were just around the corner. If they hadn't quite made it to a universal Utopia, at least they seemed to be on the right road. Ultimately they might even stop the Vietnam War and see a world at peace.

Tommy woke up suddenly. A young policeman was banging on his passenger door. Tommy got ready for the familiar ritual.

The copper wasn't about to start anything. 'You all right, mate?'

'Yeah,' said Tommy. 'I got a bit tired driving.'

'If you need to kip there's a lay-by about half-a-mile up the road.'

'Gotcher,' said Tommy, putting the van into gear. 'Thanks, mate.'

And he drove to the lay-by, wondering if pulling in at all had been a mistake. They hadn't stopped here the first time they went to Glastonbury.

They hadn't planned on this long journey.

CHAPTER TWO

Alternative Routes

He moved through the fair, smiling vaguely, greeting old acquaintances, pausing at stalls to inspect anything which resembled a map. All the regulars knew him. Most welcomed him, but others were impatient with his obsession and dismissed his quietly intense questions. Some were convinced he'd murdered his family. A lot believed privately that Joany had simply got tired of living with a loony.

Tommy kept listening to the music from the stage. He was hoping to hear what he had heard that first time, as they stood on the crest of the Tor, wondering at the sudden silence, the sense of expectation. The music, they thought, had been nothing more than a penny whistle, a Celtic drum and high, melodic voices.

They had begun the climb in darkness, somehow avoiding all barriers, all witnesses, the kids scrambling up ahead while Tommy and Joany followed, hand in hand. They planned to watch the sun rise.

They had half-expected to be stopped. In the silver pre-dawn light they paused on the path to look back. There were camps down there which they didn't recognise. Morning smoke was mingling with the thick mist. Tommy thought he heard horses. Harness.

There was no sign of the festival. They might have been the only human beings in the world. Tommy sniffed at the scented, dew-laden grass and lush foliage, looking up just as the first rays touched the chapel stones. The ruin was in better condition than he expected. He glanced around. The children were just out of sight. He heard Joany call to them, drawing their attention to the view.

The water was everywhere now. A wide, glinting marsh, from which birds rose suddenly, their wings noisy against the warming air.

[185]

Tommy thought he saw a small boat moving against the reeds. There were what looked like thatched out-buildings raised on platforms above the water. He saw no roads, no real buildings. Apart from the hills, nothing was familiar.

'Joany?'

There was a quick, unfamiliar pulse in his head, a chill in his bones.

'Joany?'

'It's amazing, isn't it,' she said. 'Now I know why they said the view was worth it. Nothing's changed!'

She was excited, throughly at ease with what was beginning to. alarm Tommy. The mist from the water rose around the base of the Tor like a tide, creating this eerie illusion. He remembered coming into Yarmouth years before, when a sea-fog filled the streets, wiping out the new concrete and emphasising the old, red brick, so that the entire town looked as it had been at the height of its Edwardian success. It was odd. He couldn't distinguish as much as a power line. Pulling himself together he turned to look up. The kids were staring at the tower and wondering if they were allowed to go in. Joany was just behind them. She turned enquiringly to Tommy.

He spread his hands. He had understood the place to be National Trust which you could only officially visit at certain times. But there were no notices, no signs or warnings, no fences.

Butch was pressing his grubby fists against an oiled oak door whose hinges, of beaten iron, glinted like new. Climbing closer to the tower, Tommy admired the restoration job. He hadn't realised they had done so much. It was very different from the outline you saw below. It seemed much slenderer, and there was an extraordinary glow to the limestone. The oriental origins of the Gothic style were obvious. The doorway was as beautiful as anything Tommy had seen in Granada or Marrakech. The windows' rich stained glass burned with vibrant light.

'Whoever built this place really loved it,' said Joany. 'I didn't realise it was so recent, did you?'

'I'll have to take a guide book out when we get home,' Tommy said. 'It's an amazing building.' He was tearful with enthusiasm. 'Look how that roof curves, the cut of the slate, and the stonework. Imagine the skill of the blokes who made all this!'

'It's like a story,' Joany followed the carving around the tower, where it joined the roof, 'people on quests and stuff. Some of those King Arthur nuts probably paid for it.' She knew a lot more about architecture than he did. 'It's no older than the oldest pre-Raphaelite! But it's the work of real artists, you can tell. See, the glass has the

[186]

same style – and it's in scenes. Joseph of Arimathea, I'd guess. And Sir Percival, or someone like him. And the Grail, of course, it's in all seven of these windows. Some romantic Birmingham ironmaster or Liverpool soap-maker commissioned this. There's a William Morris design like it at the V and A. Blimey! That cross must be pure gold!'

The crimson sun had touched the spire. Tommy guessed there were strips of brass and copper in the roof. It seemed blood streamed down all four quadrants. The cross was unfamiliar, probably Celtic, possibly pagan, hard to see. The sun was above the horizon now, flecking the ruby water with skipping gold and silver. The pole houses were black outlines. Figures moved on the platforms, getting into little boats. A light breeze rippled the water. The whole scene blazed, almost blinding him.

Tommy was still waiting for the mist to clear and reveal the evidence of civilisation when Butch shouted, 'It opens, Mum!' and slipped inside the unlatched door, Liz at his heels.

Joany dived after them, but the door was hard to push wider and she was still trying to struggle in when Tommy arrived. 'Give it a push, love, I'm stuck.'

Tommy found that the door moved easily under his hand. 'You must have loosened it up, like a jar top,' he said as they entered. 'Don't touch anything, you two.'

It was a relief not to be looking at that weird landscape.

Tommy was fond of saying that he didn't have a mystical bone in his body. He had never been interested in all that crap about Arthur and Glastonbury and ley-lines. But if that was what inspired the pre-Raphaelites to build this, it must have had something going for it.

As they got used to the jewelled gloom of the chapel, the kids fell silent with delight. Rustling silk banners, embroidered in extraordinary colours, hung from a central brass bracket suspended over a small altar of carved granite worked with silver, gold, iron and copper. The blazing windows, the richest glass Tommy had ever seen, were even more impressive from within, showing what he took to be various aspects of the Grail legend. With their intricate detail and accuracy of observation, the postures of the stylised figures displaying enormous meaning, they were the work of a master artist, with a powerful, indefinable spiritual content Tommy had never noticed in ordinary church art.

In Brookgate, where Tommy came from, near the old Sweden Street Market, most pre-war churches had been bombed and the new ones had never interested him. After his first tab of acid, at fourteen, he'd never needed an old building for a buzz.

Tommy noticed a goblet standing on the altar. By the style of the designs around the rim, it was probably Jewish, though there were also Romano-Celtic motifs, now that he looked, and even Anglo Saxon, and what might be Sanskrit and Chinese. The whole design was surprisingly coherent. He couldn't believe the Trust allowed something so valuable to be unprotected. The workmanship made it priceless, but the precious metals and gems alone were worth a million in cold cash.

The precision achieved with simple tools always amazed him. 'It must be a fake,' he said.

'What?' Joany was irritated by his interruption of the silence.

'The cup – the goblet there.'

She turned, frowning. 'What bloody cup?'

And then Butch had run up to the altar and was reaching for it.

Tommy controlled his impulse to shout. 'Better not, Butchy,' he said evenly. 'It would take a lot of pocket money to repair that!' But Liz, younger and less responsive, was now also grabbing up at the cup.

'What are you talking about,' said Joany. 'There's nothing there.'

'You're barmy,' said Tommy. 'It's not exactly an Ovaltine mug. I bet this place is normally locked. We're probably trespassing.'

'You're suddenly very respectful of private property.' But she was grave. 'It is beautiful. It would be horrible if somebody vandalised it.'

Tommy crossed to the altar and picked up a protesting Lizzy as she struggled to put her tiny hands on the cup.

'What on earth's got into you?' said Joany. 'Don't spoil it, Tom. We're not doing any harm.'

'Maybe it's a fake,' said Tommy. 'In which case it's still amazing. I'm just worried they'll think we were trying to pinch it.'

She snatched Liz from him. 'What have you been smoking?'

Liz was quiet. Her eyes over Joan's shoulder were fixed on the goblet. Butch had a similar expression. He was smiling.

Tommy Beck sighed and turned to look up at the windows, the intricate stone, the delicately carved wood worked with precious metals. 'If all churches were like this,' he said, 'you couldn't keep me out of them. We'll have to come back here, Joan.'

'As long as you don't start having visions,' she said. She shifted Liz onto her other side and took his arm. 'Are you really nervous some-one'll do us for trespass? It's a church. They're supposed to be open to everybody.'

'I don't want to spoil the holiday. We came for the music, remember.' Then Tommy screwed up his face at a sound, like a human voice's highest, loudest vibrato. 'Christ! Some sort of alarm system. Come on everyone!' He got to the door and pulled it back. Joany and Liz went first, but Butch was slow. Tommy could hardly see. Security shutters were probably coming down. 'Hurry up, lad.'

They were outside, with the door slammed behind them, before Tommy realised Butch had pinched the cup.

He tried the latch. He pushed at the heavy oak. It had locked.

'I suppose we might as well just sit here now and wait for the police.' Tommy was bitter.

When he looked, he hoped that at least the water would be gone.

The water was still there. Only the village had vanished.

CHAPTER THREE

Heavy Traffic

Tommy had no problem getting on to the Tor. He knew the whole area intimately, by night, by day, by the seasons. He could tell if a particular stone had been disturbed or a patch of wild-flowers failed to reseed. He was protective of the Tor. The Tor was his way back to Joany and the kids, to that moment when they had heard a soft humming sound, like a bee-swarm, and had gone round to the eastern side of the tower, Butch in the lead with his treasure held to his chest, and had seen the tall figure, thin as a Masai, her brooding eyes on the goblet, smiling at them, beckoning them forward. The humming now sounded human, and there was a pipe again, and a drum. A long way off . . . This woman was probably with a band . . .

The tall woman had a slender spear in her hand. She turned the spear and it seemed to expand, grow wider, until it formed a narrow doorway which opened on to teeming colour, swiftly changing shapes, an impression of myriad order, through which wound, like a moonbeam, a great silver road. Far away ahead on the road, tiny figures came and went as casually as if they strolled in Sweden Street on a Saturday afternoon. And there were other moonbeams, other roads, winding through that tapestry of restless colour. It was as if, suddenly, he was permitted a glimpse of actuality, a vision of wholeness.

The air reeked of roses and vanilla.

Tommy had felt a painful yearning, as if recollecting a forgotten loss. Even as Butch ran past the woman and through the gateway, brandishing the cup like a passport, Tommy was overcome with euphoria, a feeling of intense optimism as he realised the implications of what he seen through that opening in the fabric of his own, small sphere of reality.

'No, Liz!' Joany went after the little girl. Now all three were through, staring ahead. The tall woman smiled and beckoned to Tommy. It was as if she could only keep the gate open for a little while.

Tommy looked into the teeming possibilities of suprareality and he suddenly hesitated. 'Better not,' he had said as the woman stepped through her own gateway, drew the spear back to her body and vanished.

Tommy closed his eyes, as if to dismiss a bad dream. When he opened them the water had gone. The landscape was familiar and modern. Everything was perfectly normal. He was alone.

Tommy's shout of agony had been heard across Glastonbury.

Twenty-four years later, Tommy Beck stood with his back against the cold stones of the ruined chapel and prayed that he would stare down through the mist and see wide water glinting. Far away, someone was tapping a drum to the thin sound of a penny whistle.

Standing where they had emerged from the door, Tommy began to retrace their steps round to the eastern side, where the sun was crimson against the pale blue horizon, where the woman with the spear had opened a gateway which Tommy had been too slow to enter.

For twenty-three years Tommy Beck had stood here at exactly the same time, trying to reproduce exactly the same movements, in exactly the same conditions which had granted them their original vision of the moonbeam road and then separated them.

'There's only one problem, old dear,' said a voice from the other side of the wall. 'You haven't got the Grail any more, have you? I've had the devil of a job tracking you down. I thought you lived in Brookgate.'

'I haven't lived in Brookgate for nearly thirty years.' Tommy controlled his fear. He hated mind-games. This bloke sounded like a weirdo, a sadist, maybe.

'I frequently fall down on the fine tuning.' The speaker stepped from around the wall. 'Well, you know, it's not exactly time travel we do, but that comes into it. I get confused. I have a message. Are you interested in resuming your relationship with your wife Joan and your kids Benjamin and Elizabeth?'

Tommy could only nod. He realised he had given up hope. This could be some foul practical joke.

The pale-haired messenger was dressed in sixties revival long, tight-waisted jacket, flared trousers and a frilly shirt. All the dandified aspects of the period. Tommy hated everything the style stood for.

'You look like an old crack dealer,' he said. 'I don't do that stuff. I didn't ask for any help in this.'

'I was looking for you,' declared the dandy. 'But I went a bit out of my way. I had no intention of getting up your nose. In any way.'

'I think you'd better bugger off.' Tommy was wild with despair.

'Don't worry about them,' said the dandy, looking down at the still village. 'Their superstitions tend to work in our favour.'

From somewhere under his coat, the stranger produced a sword of dark, glowing iron. 'Eternity awaits you.'

He added: 'You'll need the cup. It's in that black plastic bag at your feet. Go on, open it. You'll see it, if I can't. It's in your blood.'

As Tommy Beck bent to pick up the Grail, the dandy lifted the heavy sword high above his head.

'Excalibur,' he explained.

CHAPTER FOUR

Abandoned Vehicle

The festival had been over a week before the police had time to trace the ownership of the abandoned Transit van.

Eventually a constable turned up in Sporting Club Square, Hammersmith, looking for a Mr Thomas Beck and was told by Beck's flatmates that Tommy had gone to Glastonbury and had never returned.

They also described Tommy's obsession, which they described as freak-burn, and when the officer passed this on to the sergeant and the sergeant had passed the report back to Somerset, Tommy was assumed to have wandered off with some bunch of like-minded loonies. There was nothing remarkable about his disappearance. He would turn up soon enough. They always did.

*

There's a road between the worlds which shimmers and curves like an erratic moonbeam. It carries a multitude of travellers. Those of us able to walk such roads, and move back and forth at will across the myriad dimensions of existence, call this particular path The Grail. From a distance off, it resembles a mighty cup.

These paths are reproduced over and over again, in millions of scales, each slightly different, yet each a detailed version of the other. They weave the fabric of the multiverse together. They are the means by which human intercourse is achieved and the soul, as well as the species, sustained.

Ordinary people walk these roads. For them Time is not a linear medium and Space has a thousand dimensions. They live to taste the textures and music of the multiverse. They live to explore their experience and to share their wisdom with anyone who desires it. They are entirely purposeful. Their spirits are rich beyond our imagining. They are fully and immortally alive.

Other species have also come to inhabit the roads between the worlds. Many follow migratory paths, making long, difficult journeys between entire universes. Some use the roads only briefly, like the lemmings, the reindeer, or the birds which every year fly between Earth and the Moon. Some, like those who investigate the darkest depths of our struggling world, are forever restless, forever seeking fresh roads through myriad scales of space and time.

Such creatures call themselves the Just and they exist to make our noblest dreams come true.